THE
JUDAS
LAWYER

THE
JUDAS
LAWYER

David Crump

QP BOOKS

New Orleans, Louisiana

Published in 2016 by QP Books, an imprint of Quid Pro Books.

ISBN 978-1-61027-368-8 (paperback)
ISBN 978-1-61027-369-5 (eBook)

QP BOOKS
Quid Pro, LLC
5860 Citrus Blvd., suite D-101
New Orleans, Louisiana 70123
www.qpbooks.com

qp

Cataloging-in-Publication Data

Crump, David.

The Judas Lawyer / David Crump.

p. cm.

ISBN 978-1-61027-368-8 (pbk.)

1. Trials—United States—Fiction. 2. Law Firms—United States—Fiction. I. Title.

PS3540.R3912C2 2016

873' .21.4—dc21

2016779324

CIP

Then Judas Iscariot, one of the twelve, went to the chief priests to betray Him to them. And when they heard it, they were glad, and promised to give him money. So he sought how he might conveniently betray Him.

Mark 14:10-11 (New Living Translation)

Author's Preface

Fictional stories about lawyers are almost never about lawyers. Not really. They usually don't show the law the way it is, or lawyers doing what they really do.

For example, some of my prepublication readers didn't know that a lawyer often sues more than one defendant in a single lawsuit. Sometimes a lawyer sues dozens of them. The readers also didn't know that lawyers on opposite sides sometimes form alliances. A plaintiff and a defendant may gang up on another defendant, or another plaintiff. And sometimes they try to keep these alliances secret. Then, the target of the alliance may get blindsided—and betrayed. These tactics really test the fairness of our system, but readers don't ever see them.

Well, this book is different.

It shows the law the way it really is. It shows lawyers mudwrestling with problems about what to put in the suit papers and how to do pretrial questioning in what are called "depositions." It shows them using expert witnesses, selecting jurors, and conducting settlement negotiations, in ways that mirror real lawsuits.

Of course, fiction is supposed to be more exciting than the boring moments in life. And so novelists use what is called "dramatic compression." Multiple characters get reduced to one, and events with lots of steps become shorter. This novel is no exception.

Even so, my story is reflective of reality. And I've added a Postscript at the end to sort out what is typical from what is not. This part of the book will help you to separate the real from the imaginary.

But now, it's time to get into our story. Imagine that you are a new lawyer. You've gone to work at a firm called Robert Herrick and Associates. You are about take part in a big piece of litigation, with plenty of twists and turns. And all you have to do is turn the page.

THE
JUDAS
LAWYER

1

The buzzer sounded. It came from inside the jury room, to signal a verdict. Its sharp tone shot across the courtroom, and then it lingered, full of promise and danger.

"I'm not sure about this case at all," Robert Herrick whispered. He closed his eyes and pushed back a shock of dark hair. His blue eyes were clouded with worry.

"Neither am I." Tom Kennedy was Robert's closest partner, the one he worked with most often. "It started with the other plaintiffs' lawyers looking like they were defense lawyers. They trashed us, and themselves, in the way they struck the jurors. They removed people that were ideal for a plaintiff."

"And the questions these so-called plaintiffs' lawyers asked? Those questions were aimed at pinning the blame on us, a fellow plaintiff, instead of on the defendants."

"It looks like an under-the-table deal. I mean, the other plaintiffs' lawyers have been constantly agreeing with the defense. Against us."

"But of course they denied that they had a deal to combine against us. Or any agreement."

Judge Manny Lopez had climbed to the bench. "Bring in the jury."

Across the courtroom, Jimmy Coleman stood up. He was short, about five foot nine, but powerful: a no-holds-barred brawler who had fought Robert in so many cases. His brownish-white hair was combed straight back, and he didn't smile; he smirked. He wore a map of his life on his face, with eyes so pale and dead that witnesses turned away when Jimmy cross-examined them.

1

A gaggle of junior lawyers stood beside Jimmy, all wearing black suits. That was the uniform at the huge, factory-like firm of Booker and Bayne. None of these junior mouthpieces had done anything during the trial, but Jimmy always brought an entourage.

Robert and Tom stood too. The jurors shuffled in, slowly. They did not look at the plaintiffs' lawyers or at the man in the wheelchair beside them.

"That's a bad sign." Robert cringed as he pulled himself to his full six-foot-two height to see the last juror. The collar of his hundred-fifty-dollar shirt pulled at his neck, under his pin-striped suit. He felt sweat covering it, then running down his back.

Usually, women jurors loved him instantly. Usually, the men were impressed with his ability to confess the difficulties in his case, without confessing weakness, and to speak powerfully at the end of a hard case without notes.

But not these jurors, it seemed.

"They look unhappy, these folks." Tom shook his head. "They look like people who've made a difficult decision. Such as . . . the decision to leave a plaintiff out in the cold, when they know he's hurt."

"Ladies and gentlemen of the jury, have you reached a verdict?" Judge Lopez was an elegant man, with meticulously placed hair and a glen plaid suit under his robe. He smiled at the jurors. After all, they would be voters during the election that was coming soon, and he was running for re-election, as judges did in this state.

"Yes, we have a verdict, your Honor." It was spoken by the presiding juror, a figure with military posture, whom Robert and Tom recognized as a retired marine colonel.

"Pass the charge and verdict form to the bailiff, please." The entire process seemed to float in slow motion. Deliberately, Judge Lopez unfolded the papers. More deliberately, he stared at the jury's answers to the questions.

He slowed, at one point, and frowned, when he was about a quarter of the way through. Must be the crucial question about who was negligent, Robert thought miserably.

It struck him hard, suddenly. "I just know the defendants and the other plaintiffs had one of those no-deal deals," he whispered to Tom. "They cooperated, but they did it all by winks and nods, without communicating by words."

Tom nodded. "I think so too. They all knew that if these other two plaintiffs put the blame on our guy, the defendants would take care of them. And ensure that they came out all right. All arranged silently."

The judge was still checking the jury's answers, with a puzzled look on his face. At one point, he lifted the document and looked at it from underneath, for no apparent reason.

"The . . . verdict seems to be in order," Judge Lopez announced quietly.

Every lawyer in the courtroom was thinking, "Come on! *What* is the verdict, your Honor? Come on!"

Finally, the judge started reading out loud. "Whose negligence, if any, was a proximate cause of the occurrence in question?"

He hesitated, then, before saying, "And the jury answered, 'The Blackminster Construction Company, Gunther Blackminster, and the Janowitz Company.'"

So far, so good, Robert thought. Those were the defendants.

"And William Grant," said the judge. "The plaintiff. The jury found *him* negligent too." That was unexpected, and the judge read it in a way that signaled his own surprise.

This was Robert and Tom's client. The man in the wheelchair. William Grant, the plaintiff. Robert had already moved to stand beside William, with his hand on the man's shoulder.

As soon as the judge said it, the courtroom reverberated with a shrill sound of surprise, a moan, from the audience. The judge wore pain on his face.

"The next question for the jury," Judge Lopez read on, "was, 'What percentage of negligence is attributable to each of the persons found by you to have been negligent?'"

This was the key question. In a system that lawyers call "comparative negligence," the percentages of blame that the jury puts on each party determine what percentage the plaintiff recovers of his damages. If anything.

The judge cleared his throat and stared at the verdict. "And the jury answered, 'Blackminster Construction Company, twenty percent. Gunther Blackminster, zero. Janowitz Company, twenty percent.'"

Robert felt the acid in his stomach moving into his throat.

The judge stared, hesitated, and then read, "And William Grant, the plaintiff, sixty percent."

The courtroom was stone silent. But at the defendants' table, Jimmy Coleman's dirty teeth showed as he smiled. And his smile widened, above a jaw with a formidable set of jowls. One of the black-suited associates whispered, "We did it," loudly enough to be heard across the courtroom.

The judge paused, took off his glasses, and then put them back on. "It's . . . a defense verdict, as to William Grant. It's zero for him. If a plaintiff is anything over fifty percent negligent, that plaintiff recovers nothing, in this state. Nothing."

That's right, Robert thought, dumfounded. We recover nothing. William Grant, whose life had taken such a terrible turn in that instant caused by these guilty-as-sin defendants, would recover nothing to compensate for his lost livelihood, his medical expenses, or the pain he would suffer for the rest of his life.

The judge read on. But to Robert and Tom, the rest hardly mattered. The two other plaintiffs recovered handsomely. Hundreds of thousands of dollars each. Enough so that they would collect more than their real damages, even though the defendants were only forty percent to blame.

Now, the judge was reading the question about damages for William Grant. Robert and Tom's client. "And the jury answered, 'William Grant, zero damages,'" said the judge.

The judge polled the jurors, asking whether the verdict was agreed to by each one. He thanked them and excused them. Then, he turned to the defense lawyer and said, curtly, "Mr. Coleman, draft me a final judgment."

Jimmy was smiling and nearly dancing. He looked as though he had swallowed a gallon of Red Bull. "Certainly, your Honor. Later today, and it will come by messenger."

The community of lawyers knew that Jimmy Coleman had grown up in Los Angeles and had been a gang member as a teenager. But everyone wondered how this primitive boy had graduated from college and from the law school at UCLA, and how he had risen to the leadership in a respected international law firm.

"All right." The judge spoke in a subdued voice. "Everyone is excused."

There was a lot of shuffling as lawyers shoehorned papers into too-small Redrope file pockets and headed for the door. Robert just sat for a moment, thinking what to say to William Grant, besides saying, "We lost."

But Jimmy Coleman knew what he wanted to say. He sauntered up and stood behind Robert, beaming. "Herrick, looks like you brought a piece-of-shit case to the courthouse." Jimmy waved his arms, making his light blue Italian sport jacket rise up around his neck. "But thanks for giving us a whole lot of fun."

The black-suited Booker and Bayne associates all giggled at that.

2

The next three days were miserable, and they passed slowly. Every lawyer has gone through a period of drinking too much, or at least most lawyers have. It goes with the stress of the job, even though it is a lousy way of dealing with stress.

Robert Herrick was not immune from this tendency toward alcohol.

He was used to winning, but he was used to losing, too. If a lawyer tries a lot of cases, he loses some. But this case—William Grant's case—hurt more than most. His client was, in Robert's mind, blameless, and he had been hurt badly. The evidence against the defendants was strong and clear.

He shouldn't have lost this case.

But he had lost it. The contradiction twisted and turned in his mind.

His wife frowned at him. "That's your third glass of Scotch, today. And it's still morning. You need to slow down, Robert. I'm so, so worried about you."

"But it's good Scotch. Not a headache in the bottle."

Robert Herrick had left Harvard College, years ago, with his degree, and joined the Marines. A few years later, he graduated from law school at the University of Houston. He had turned down offers from all the elite firms in town because he wanted to go it alone.

His wife knew that his dedication to his clients had made his reputation, but now, she knew he was feeling it too much. "Baby, I'm worried about you."

"I'm worried about me too, but I'm more worried about William Grant."

His wife was Maria Melendes, and she was an assistant district attorney. A prosecutor. She had a stressful job too. She didn't remind him of that very often, but now she was about to.

"Remember that murder case I prosecuted a few years ago? The evidence was definitely there. It was powerful. The witnesses were solid citizens, and they testified without any kind of contradiction in what they said. The defendant claimed self-defense because, supposedly, the victim made what that killer called a 'hip pocket motion.'"

"Yes. I remember it. And of course, the last ditch defense of a lying defendant is to claim that the other guy made a so-called hip pocket motion, and therefore this wasn't a murder. It was self-defense."

"Only it obviously wasn't, in this case. The physical evidence made self-defense impossible, the way the defendant told about it."

"Yes. I remember all of that."

"The defendant's story was ludicrous and desperate. But . . . ."

"I remember."

". . . but he was acquitted."

"I remember."

"The jury just decided to let him go. There wasn't enough proof, they said. The evidence was overwhelming, but still, there wasn't enough proof, according to those twelve half-wits. And Robert, this case of yours with William Grant can't be any worse than that was."

"No. But Maria, you were upset, just like me."

The ringing of the telephone interrupted them. Maria went to answer it. Robert drained the third glass of Scotch and got up to pour another one.

The law firm he had founded now numbered twenty-eight lawyers, who fought in favor of individuals or small firms against bigger lawbreakers. All told, he had more than a hundred employees, including an audio-visual department that made videos and charts for use in court. He had been president of the Bar Association, a member of a blue ribbon committee appointed by the Supreme Court to revise the practice, and the leader of efforts among local lawyers to provide legal service to the poor.

But none of that mattered now, he thought to himself, as he forgot the ringing telephone.

* * *

It seemed like a long time before Maria called him. He wasn't thinking about anything in particular. He only thought about the switch in his head that he was trying to trip. The one that would interrupt that awful feeling of loss.

Finally, he heard Maria saying his name. As if from far away, but urgent.

"Robert! Come here. It's Tom Kennedy. William Grant has tried to commit suicide."

He tripped over the edge of the couch on the way to the telephone.

* * *

It was three days later before he finally was able to meet personally with his client, William Grant.

"William, you've got a lot of life left in you."

"It doesn't feel that way."

The injured man still sat in his wheelchair, but both of his hands were covered with gauze. Instead of saying anything about the incident, William's wife had wordlessly given him a copy of a hospital report, just a few pages of the full chart. "The patient presented with cuts on both wrists. History is that he lost a jury trial and feels responsible to his family for having lost it. This, plus depression, plus his injuries from the prior accident, contributed to his condition. No history of suicidal ideation, or earlier attempts, or statements about suicide."

Unusual, Robert thought. The most frequent indicator of suicide is depression, but most people who are depressed don't commit suicide. The next strongest indicators are earlier attempts, suicidal statements, and suicidal "ideation," or in other words, thinking about it and planning a method. But none of these appeared in William Grant's case. It made Robert feel even worse than he had earlier, because it meant that the loss at trial had had an exaggerated effect on William's desperate move.

"William," he said firmly, "you didn't lose that case. Your lawyers did."

"But I was there, and I thought you were ahead all the way, Robert."

"Sometimes it's just the fault of a bad jury. Justice is the most difficult thing on earth to predict, especially with a jury."

"The jury somehow didn't believe me."

"Or me."

William Grant's eyes misted for a moment. Then, he said, slowly, "What is left to do? Is there anything? Can we go back to court? Can we appeal?"

Robert didn't answer for a moment. The prospects were so poor for those kinds of efforts. You could go back to the trial judge, but jury verdicts were not something that trial judges tampered with easily. Could he make a credible Motion for New Trial? You can file that motion, but it's a long shot—a very long shot. Could there be a successful appeal? That was a long shot, too. If the plaintiff loses a jury trial in this state, he reflected, there's usually not an appeal at all, because the odds are heavily against success.

But he knew what he needed to say to William Grant.

"Yes. We will file a Motion for New Trial, William. Yes, we will. And if that doesn't work, yes, we will appeal."

He was surprised by his own vehemence in promising these things.

He looked straight into his client's eyes. "Meanwhile, William, keep yourself healthy. Don't do anything like this again. I don't want you to commit suicide. I want you to live. Promise me. I'm promising you, we will keep fighting."

What bystanders can do if suicide is in the air, besides obtaining professional therapy, is to express strong wishes against it.

The man in the wheelchair just looked down for a few seconds. His voice was barely audible when he said, simply, "Okay."

As Robert pulled on his coat to leave, and after he had said his goodbyes, he went over the case in his mind. Where had the course of the trial taken bad enough turns so that a Motion for New Trial or an appeal might work?

And as he thought back over the two years since he had met William Grant, he said to himself, How did we get to this point?

Where did this loss, in this case, really begin?

3

wo years earlier . . .

The injured man who was Robert Herrick's client, William Grant, had started his working life as a hod carrier. A union worker on the lowest rung of the ladder. They called him Little Willie at the job site, even though he was a big man with blazing red hair, because he was the lowliest kind of assistant. He did what he was told, and soon Little Willie Grant was climbing the ranks to better and better jobs. As a construction foreman, he worked closely with the union and earned a reputation for straight dealing.

By age forty-five, William Grant was a vice president of his company, the Worley Construction Company. He was still called Little Willie, even if it didn't fit. He occupied an office next to Steve Worley and Tim Worley. He had made it on merit, in this family corporation.

It wasn't easy making the switch to the management side. Of course, he had worn the company hat as a foreman, but that job had meant he was still close to the men. Now, he was solidly removed from his roots. The union guys kidded him: "You were the Bruce Jenner of this outfit, only now you're Caitlyn Jenner since you switched over to the other side." But it was good-natured kidding. William Grant knew his place, which was with the company, but the working men realized he'd never forgotten where he'd come from.

And the company valued his connections at the job site. He was there frequently, seeing who was working the way he should, whether the job site complied with OSHA regulations, and who or what was making trouble. He went together with the inside architect and, usually, another company man, who changed from job to job. It was Willie, the architect, and whoever else came, as top men from the company.

* * *

On a Tuesday, Willie got a message. "Meeting in the conference room at ten o'clock." As he walked in, Steve and Tim Worley both grinned at him.

"I've got some good news and some bad news, Willie," Steve said.

"Give me the good news first," Willie grinned too.

"We've been tapped to take over part of the work on a skyscraper that Shell is building. The Shell people had a lot of trouble with the original contractor, and they came to us to replace that company. This job is a big deal. It'll put us on the map."

"That's great! . . . But what's the bad news?"

"It's in Anchorage. The construction job is in Anchorage."

"Anchorage?"

"Anchorage, Alaska."

"Alaska?"

"And the only person who can really supervise this job is . . . you, Willie."

"*Anchorage, Alaska?*"

"Yes. We need you to go there."

Silence. Then Willie wanted to know: "What's Anchorage, Alaska gonna be like this time of year?"

"Cold, but not all that cold. I looked into it, soon as I saw we needed to send you. In summer, the weather is mild, around 50 to just under 80 degrees. It's warmed up by ocean currents."

"Well, but . . . it's winter now."

"Okay. 5 degrees to 40 degrees for a couple of months in the winter. But hey, you can see the aurora borealis. You know, those wavy colors that dance across the sky."

"Great."

"And it's a good sized, sophisticated city. More than 300,000 population. Kind of like Omaha or Tucson."

"Great." He paused. "But . . . hey! Isn't this the famous 'Land of the Midnight Sun?'"

"Not exactly."

"And that means that there's sun later at night in summer, but in winter, there's darkness during the day. Like, it's really 'the Land of Night during Daytime.' That'd be a better name for it: *The Land of Night during Daytime.*"

"Not exactly. Well, maybe some of the winter. The tilt of the earth does it. It gets dark and stays dark a few months, but there are a few hours of sun most days."

"Great."

"Willie, this isn't Point Barrow, Alaska. That's the farthest north town in the United States, many hundreds of miles north of Anchorage, which is in south Alaska. Man, it's cold, cold in Point Barrow. But Anchorage isn't like that. It's actually pretty temperate. Not like what people usually think of, when they think about Alaska."

"Great."

"Look, Willie. Take your wife. Take Delores. I know you two are inseparable. Stay at a nice hotel. From what I understand, they've actually got a lot of nice hotels in Anchorage. It's a sophisticated city, and it hosts a lot of big shot oil folks." Steve Worley grinned again. "And also, it hosts big shots like you, Willie."

Tim Worley grinned too. "We appreciate you, Willie. You're sure a big shot around here, to us. That's why you're the right guy for this job."

4

The Land of the Midnight Sun. Or, the Land of Night during Daytime. Actually, Anchorage wasn't quite like that. Willie had been here two months now. It had been so, so cold for him. The icy feeling bit into his skin no matter how thick his coat was. And it was even colder for Delores. The sun was out for a too-short time in the middle of the day, and it got dark really early.

Today was a dark, dark night—at six o'clock in the afternoon. The stars were like tiny, shining crystals on the black velvet sheet of the sky. The project went on, in the dark, because it was still daytime, with a hundred football-field lights all around. The girders of the building's first floor were complete, and a few more spires stretched up toward the night-like day. This particular day would be Willie's last site visit, although no one knew that. The steel skeleton of a 22-story building-to-be was just getting into its third floor. The elevator was on its way up, and the crane was on its way down.

"Coming around," the cry went out. "Coming around!" The hundredweight crane was swinging in a circle, not the tallest crane that would be used at the top stories when the structure got there, but tall enough to look serious. The hook at the end was swinging and bouncing around in the wind. Willie and the architect and another company man were standing in a dusty embankment at the opposite end of the site, a patch of open land that would become grass and gardens when the job was complete. Far enough away so that none of them could hear the warning, "Coming around!"

Inexplicably, the operator lowered the hook to the ground. Unexpectedly, he swung it far beyond where it was supposed to go. And strangely, he snapped it back upward. Maybe, everyone speculated later, he had figured out that he had overshot the mark and was trying to right his target. Or, he just didn't know what he was doing, which was entirely possible, because this operator was a rookie.

Willie had his back to the structure, facing away from the crane. He and the other two men were climbing out of the job site. But before they got away, the hook traveled beyond them, swung out, swung back, and grabbed Willie. It tore into his abdomen and traveled up into his sternum. As one eyewitness said later, "The point of that hook cut him almost in two. That sucker gutted Little Willie like a fish. He was cut like a brook trout."

The hook continued its travels and injured the other two men too. The architect's arm was broken. The other company man had lacerations to his face and a broken cheekbone.

Willie flopped onto the ground sideways, in a fetal position. Quickly, mercifully, he was unconscious. Drifting into shock. Within seconds, the men on the safety squad had him on a stretcher with his legs elevated and were trying to stop the bleeding. An ambulance was already on the way. At the hospital, the intake physician triaged him to bypass a horde of uninsured patients with sniffles and scrapes, and fast hands lifted him onto an operating table with a series of shouts for blood, antibiotics, and instruments. Anchorage was familiar with serious injuries from the shoreline—from on board ships, and in the oil patch, and it had good hospitals. But Willie's injuries were visible, red, and spectacular, and no one was sure he would survive.

* * *

He did survive, but survive was all he did. He wore a broad scar and would always need a wheelchair or walk painfully, with a debilitated limp. Infections had required a series of different surgeries, and his small intestine was confused. He lost thirty-five pounds and no longer wanted to play pool or go to football games.

After three days in an Alaskan hospital, he was a shadow of himself, but he was stable enough to travel home by air ambulance. Not to go to his home, but to go to a bigger hospital. The Medical Center of Houston, clustered around Main, Fannin, and Holcombe Streets, was a major asset of the city. Health care and hospitals ranked right up there with the space and oil industries. The Med Center had the finest cancer hospital in the world: the M.D. Anderson Cancer Center. It had one of the best Heart Institutes, which was a joint effort of CHI St. Luke's Hospitals and Baylor Medical School. It had a star-quality trauma center at Ben Taub Hospital. And on and on.

The Med Center was, indeed, a city unto itself. It had its own power sources, in case the city's electricity cut off. It had dozens of spires that held hotels, doctors' offices, stores, restaurants, and, of course, hospitals. The Med Center was also a beehive of activity: of growth and change. Construction cranes were everywhere, and they seemed to multiply, with more towers always reaching skyward.

Willie was here for weeks on end. Weeks that seemed like years. Methodist Hospital had multiple intensive care units, and Willie ended up in the ICU designated "Other," meaning that his injuries didn't fit any of the usual life-threatening categories. Whenever he looked out the window, he could see two nearby construction cranes, or at times, three. At first, he looked away whenever he caught a glimpse of them, and even later, he never got used to the sight.

The day he finally was discharged, his wife came with balloons, ribbons, and flowers. Delores took him home. The house had been adapted, with a different bed and different furniture.

It wasn't long before Willie and Delores figured that they ought to go see a lawyer. They called the most reliable guide that they could think of for that, who was the union steward, of course. "Willie, you got to go see this lawyer named Robert Herrick," the man said. "H-e-r-r-i-c-k. He's the well-known 'Lawyer for the Little Guy,' and he's not like a lawyer. He's more like one of us. And you got a good case. Yeah, you done lost a lot, but this way, I hope you can get a lot back."

* * *

In Willie's living room, there were two La-Z-Boy chairs that leaned back, a television, and a couple of side chairs. When he came to visit, since Willie couldn't easily come to him, Robert Herrick sat in one of the smaller seats.

"I'll be honest with you," he said. "That wound on your stomach looks brutal, Mr. Grant. The jury will think so too."

"I never thought we'd be doing a house calls," added Tom Kennedy. "But from what I've already heard about you, Mr. Grant, I'm proud to know you."

The man in the maneuverable bed smiled, then grimaced. "Call me Willie." His lunch, all liquid, sat on a tray that was pushed to the side. Everything but the furniture was white or off-white: the walls, the floor, and Willie's open sleepshirt.

"You've told me what happened," Robert said. "Can you give me your best guess about *why* it happened?"

"Well, I'm used to measuring my opinions. But I see you want me to guess. Realize, it's just a guess. I think it happened because the guy pulling the toggle switches on that crane was brand new."

"That could be right, from what I know."

"That crane operator worked for the Blackminster Construction Company. We hired them to operate the crane and some other stuff. Blackminster Construction, that's Gunther Blackminster's company. That guy Gunther Blackminster, he made it in this business by paying the least amount he could. Being cheap, and a lot of times, cheaper than what was needed. I'd say it finally caught up with him. Or rather, it caught up with me."

"That's right. But Willie, we're here to do something about it."

"I know. Anyway, the crane operator was new. Probably inexperienced. Gunther Blackminster chased off another guy who operated the crane just before this. So, I think that had to do with it. The guy's inexperience. And good old Gunther, he knew it."

Little Willie paused. His face wore an expression of anger and regret. "We all knew Gunther Blackminster, of course. Me and the Worleys all knew him. I asked them, in fact I begged them, not to get Gunther or Blackminster Construction into the middle of this. But Steve Worley—president of the Worley Construction Company—was like, 'We've known Gunther since all of us were wet behind the ears. Our wives go to the country club together.'

"And so I ended up having to work with Gunther Blackminster and the Blackminster Construction Company."

"Okay. And I heard something about the crane not being quite right, too."

"Well, yeah. The gears on these things stick, and that means the toggle levers don't work right. The controls. A crane requires all kinds of maintenance. It's a complicated instrument, a crane, even though people don't realize it. And that part was the fault of the Janowitz Company. That's who owned it. I mean, Janowitz Company leased the crane to us and kept it running. And the toggle controls stuck. You could handle it if you were good at it, but this little fellow, this new guy, he wasn't good enough to make it work right."

"What are your job prospects, Willie?" Tom Kennedy spoke up. He was writing notes furiously. "This is important for our lawsuit. The damages."

"I don't know if there's anything I can do." The injured man's face fell. "I can't do what I was doing for Worley Construction. Can you see me racing over dirt and debris in a wheelie machine? Or hopping up a construction elevator? So. What can I do? I don't know. I've got a high school education. And some college, but didn't graduate."

"This may sound corny, but tell us how the pain is. On a one to ten scale."

"Well, I've got all kinda meds right now. They take the edge off. But when it gets too long in between, it comes back. And it feels like someone poured red hot soup over my innards. Or melted lead."

Willie sighed. "But I'm gonna do something. Something productive, when I get out of bed. I understand the Salvation Army hires disabled folks, at maybe 99 cents an hour, to sort out coat hangers. I've got at least two more surgeries 'fore I get freed of going back to that hospital every day. That place, that . . . sanitized doghouse. They'll give me pain meds to carry 'round, and I can start looking for work. And that's when I'll find out . . . I'll find out what the pain is really like."

* * *

There was a priceless Italian chest in Jimmy Coleman's corner office. Centuries ago, a master craftsman had made this wonderful piece by the intarsiato method: by inlaying pieces intricately into it. Flowering vines of green, brown, and red spilled over every one of its light wooden surfaces, and gold hardware glittered everywhere.

Jimmy sat at a desk that had been made in Tuscany to match the chest, with the same vines and leaves. He faced his favorite associate, Jennifer Lowenstein, who sat at a desk chair that also matched the green, brown and red pattern.

"Jennifer, I got a call from Gunther Blackminster," he told her. "I don't have to tell you how fine a client Blackminster Construction Company is."

She smiled. "Of course not. We've gotten them out of a whole bunch of scrapes with the law. Sometimes without them even getting their just deserts."

"Which was justice, according to us." Jimmy laughed. "Well, anyway, Blackminster Construction Company is closer to the bankruptcy line than you'd like to hear about. In spite of having some good gigs. I think Gunther's living style and his two divorces have lightened the company's pockets. And they just had a real bad accident that hurt three people."

"They need us?"

"Yes, indeed. This is a bet-the-company situation. In spite of my having said it's a bad accident, our position is that it's not so bad."

"Of course."

"And Blackminster heard from inside the union about the guy who's worst injured. That guy has hired Robert Herrick."

"Whom we know."

"We'll just have to take him on and beat him, but we'll need to work at it."

"We can do that."

"And we need some help. We need the best judge for us, the friendliest we can get. And Jennifer, it's going to take some maneuvering to get the case sent to the court we want. So . . . Jennifer, here's what we're going to do to get us a pro-defense judge . . . ."

5

Willie's story troubled Robert more than he had expected. He'd had plenty of clients in the past who were badly injured. But it was obvious that this guy had been in great health beforehand, able to do an indoor-outdoor job with heavy pressure. It had all changed in an instant, in an unforgettable accident.

But with his thoughts still focused on Willie, he had to put on a cheerful front. Especially tonight. Tonight was a time to be happy, even if it was an act of will.

"Thank goodness we're all still able to get together." Robert Herrick beamed at his family. "We've had a dinner like this every Wednesday, with the whole clan together, for over a year, without missing."

"Which is amazing," said his wife, Maria Melendes, with a smile, "especially with your crazy schedule, Robert."

Robert smiled back and said what was customary, whether he agreed or not. "Yes, my love."

He was sitting at the head of the table, with Maria at the other end. Next to Robert was his daughter, who went by the name Pepper. "If you call her Cynthia," the saying went, "you're in trouble, even though that's her real name. She's *Pepper*." And next to her was "Little Robert," Pepper's son, so called to distinguish him from Big-Robert-the-patriarch. Across from them was Jonathan, Pepper's husband, and Pepper's brother, Robert Junior, who was called Robbie, also to minimize the confusion.

"So, Daddy," said Pepper, "you got a new case today?"

"Yes. And this plaintiff deserves to win his case. This gentleman needs help. He's hurt bad. It's an opportunity to do something good with my law degree."

"I always hope it's more than that," Maria announced. "I always hope that you've taken on a good case instead of a case that you're only going to lose. That doesn't do anybody any good. Having a pro bono instinct is good, to a point. But sometimes it takes you over, Robert, and makes you do things that don't do anyone any good."

"Yes, my dear wife."

"You've been known to do that." She smiled. "Too often."

"It's true." He smiled back. "But this case is both. It's one where I can help somebody, and it's also a good case."

"Oh, yes? Pray, tell us why it's a good case."

He described the incident and the injury. "So, as you can see, the man has huge damages, and the liability is there."

Maria smiled, but she shook her head slightly, almost imperceptibly. "Remember, my gorgeous man, that I'm a lawyer too. And in fact, I'm a trial lawyer too."

Maria was an assistant district attorney. Her cases were mostly criminal, but as she said, "Juries are juries."

"No, really," he answered, "it's a straightforward case. A simple case."

"Well . . . maybe." She sounded skeptical. "But I always wonder when anyone in my office says the case is straightforward. Or simple. You're always going to have somebody on the other side who makes the case *not* be straightforward. And who makes it *anything but* simple. I cringe whenever anyone in my office says a case is simple. When they say that, I always suspect it won't be."

He stared at her. She was beautiful, with reddish hair that hung in ringlets and pure pale Hispanic skin. Her eyes were brighter than any he had ever seen, and her smile was perfect.

And, of course . . . , she was right about what she was saying. And he knew she was right.

* * *

The lawsuit was not simple, in fact. And the very next morning, Robert saw one of the many reasons why.

"Come to think of it," he said to Tom Kennedy, "we might need to file this lawsuit in Alaska. That is, we may not be able to file it here at home, but we might have to file it in . . . Alaska."

"Because . . . that's where it happened?"

"Right."

"Possibly so. Because it all happened in Alaska. Wow, that would be a mess."

"Especially, Tom, since you and I aren't admitted to practice in Alaska, of all places."

"We'd have to hire local Alaskan lawyers to assist, and we'd have to handle a lawsuit thousands of miles away."

"Can't we file it here?" Tom brightened a little. "The defendants are here, I think. All of them. Blackminster Construction Company, Gunther Blackminster, Janowitz Company. I'll check, but I think they're all right here, in this city."

"Is our client better off here than in Alaska?"

"Well . . . sure. I can't imagine why he'd be better off with an Alaskan jury. He's from somewhere else, not Alaska, and he'd be in front of a jury of Alaskans. Nothing wrong with Alaskans, of course, but our man would be an outsider. And this is the place, here at home, where he'd get bigger damages from a home jury."

"All right. And if the defendants are here, I think we might be able to file suit here even if the events took place in Alaska."

"The Supreme Court cases about that . . . are confusing. I mean, the Court's opinions about when you can file suit about an event that happened somewhere else."

"Yes, indeed." Robert nodded. "But the Supreme Court says you can sue here, even if the events happened somewhere else, if the defendants are *'essentially at home'* here. Not very precise language, and not as good guidance as you'd think ought to be in a Supreme Court opinion. Essentially at home? What does that mean?"

"Not at all clear, no. But these defendants have their central offices here, and all their officers and directors. They're as *'essentially at home'* here as a corporation can be."

"Here's another issue. It would make our clients' heads spin. If we file suit here, does the court have to follow *Alaskan* law? And do it the way they'd do it in *Alaska*?"

"Maybe. Maybe not."

"I think it's clear." Robert had decided. "We can file suit here. We can finesse the issue, about whether Alaskan law applies. Maybe not. So, Tom, go ahead and write the suit papers."

6

Tom Kennedy sat at one of the three mahogany chairs in front of Robert Herrick's desk. "Not much difficulty in writing the suit papers for William Grant's case, once we decided to file suit here. They're easy."

"I guess that's right."

They both looked out the greenhouse-style floor-to-ceiling windows toward the west, past the greensward of Buffalo Bayou, past the big trees of Memorial Park, to the place where the horizon drifted to blue. The offices of the Herrick Firm sprawled at the top of the Chase Bank Building. The tallest structure in town.

Below the big mahogany desk, the most beautiful oriental carpet Tom had ever seen stretched out with its squares, diamonds, and triangles in every color, and ended under a forest of geraniums in red and pink.

Robert grinned. "But just because the suit papers are easy to write, that doesn't mean that everything's going to be easy in this case."

"Nothing's ever easy." And they both laughed, because unfortunately, everything in the law is always more complicated, more expensive, and more full of delay than anyone would expect.

To the south, the spires of the city grew in shades of gray, brown, and white. Down below, way down, the traffic crawled around the loops and curves and tangles of the freeway system.

Robert shook his head. "No, nothing's ever easy."

He reached across the desk. "Okay, Tom. Let me look at what you've written. The original suit papers." He scanned the document.

And what he saw was this, with all the technical elements not yet included, but otherwise ready for filing in a state district court. Here were the top ten lines:

No. _____

WILLIAM AND DELORES GRANT, Plaintiffs	**) IN THE DISTRICT**
v.	**)**
THE BLACKMINSTER CONSTRUCTION COMPANY,	**) COURT NO. ___**
GUNTHER BLACKMINSTER, AND	**)**
JANOWITZ COMPANY, Defendants	**) OF HARRIS COUNTY**

PLAINTIFFS WILLIAM AND KATHLEEN GRANT'S ORIGINAL PETITION

Robert laid the document aside momentarily. "Congratulations, Tom!" he said with mock excitement. "So far so good. The heading looks as though it's correct."

"Gee, thanks, boss man," Tom said drily.

Robert read on, past the first paragraph.

Plaintiffs are residents of Harris County. The residences of the Defendants are also Harris County. This case should be heard in Harris County because the defendants' principal offices or residence are here. Plaintiffs allege that this is a suit for monetary damages only, totaling more than $ 1 million.

"Tom, you're on a roll! This purely technical paragraph looks good too."

"Stop clowning, boss. It's unbecoming."

"All right. The next paragraphs are the real deal. This will be the part that counts."

I. THE FACTS

2. Plaintiff William Grant was working a construction job site when a huge crane came around. The crane had a hook at its end. The hook imbedded itself in Plaintiff's abdomen, ripped his body open, and caused Plaintiff severe injuries.

3. Plaintiff William Grant's damages include loss of earnings, past and future; medical expenses, past and future; physical and mental pain, past and future; and loss of consortium, companionship, advice, and solace with his wife, Kathleen Grant, past and future.

4. Kathleen Grant's damages include loss of consortium, companionship, advice, and solace with her husband, William Grant, past and future.

Robert studied these paragraphs with a little more attention. Finally, he said, "All right," and read on. The claims of negligence that came next were crucial, and Tom would have been trying to write them so they were repetitious and as broad as possible.

II. THE CLAIMS

5. The Defendants, alone and collectively, were negligent in handling the crane and hook, in all of the following respects:

> **a. in failing to guide the hook away from the body of William Grant;**
>
> **b. in causing the hook to come into contact with the body of William Grant;**
>
> **c. in using and employing a crane operator who lacked sufficient experience to operate the crane and hook in a safe manner; and**
>
> **d. in using and employing and leasing and furnishing crane and hook mechanisms that had controls that were difficult to operate;**

and all of these acts or omissions of negligence, taken singularly or together, were a proximate cause of the Plaintiff's damages.

For these reasons, Plaintiffs pray that they recover their damages as set forth above, from the Defendants, for prejudgment and postjudgment interest allowed by the law, and for such other relief, both general and special, in law and in equity, to which they may prove themselves entitled.

The signature block was blank, but they both knew what would go into it.

"You know, Tom, I always thought in law school that this kind of lawsuit would be written in some sort of archaic language that couldn't be understood. That's the fault of our professors, I guess. Your draft tells it straight out, which is the way it ought to be. Oh, I guess there's a lot of fancy language at the beginning and at the end, but it looks fine with me."

"Thanks."

"Let's get it printed out in final. And let's file it. Electronically, of course, as we always do in this county."

* * *

A moment after Tom left on his way to file the suit papers, the telephone rang. "I'm sorry, Robert." Donna deCarlo's voice came over the intercom. "It's your not-so-old, not-so friend, Jimmy Coleman."

She laughed, almost involuntarily. Robert groaned. Then he picked up the phone.

"Hello, Jimmy."

"Robert, how the hell are you?" Jimmy didn't wait for an answer. "I heard a rumor that you were studying a lawsuit that you might file on behalf of this guy named William Grant."

"Well . . . at this point I can't answer that. It would be confidential, if it were true, until we filed something."

Jimmy choked out a wet, coarse laugh. "I'll take that as a yes." He roared his half-belch, half-laugh again. "But I'd like to persuade you not to take that lawsuit on."

Tell this to a lawyer—what Jimmy was saying—and the lawyer's got to listen. The speaker might reveal some kind of helpful information. At the least, it might show what your future opponent *wanted* you to believe.

"So, tell me why you say that, Jimmy. Why you think I should refuse this lawsuit. I'm listening. I've got both ears on."

"That guy, he caused his own accident." Jimmy's voice sounded like metal grinding on concrete. "This William Grant, I mean. In the first place, everybody was screamin at him that 'the crane's comin around.' He knew what that meant. In the second place, he was in a no-man's zone—I mean, where nobody ought to be just standin around, and he knew that too—and he was just lollygaggin like a deer in the road, not payin any attention. In the third place, he turned his back completely and was clueless as a tuna fish, and that's something he knew too. What I'm tellin ya is, Herrick, this is a case that has contributory negligence written all over it, and it's a loser."

Robert knew all of this, and he knew that there were answers to all of it. But he just said, "Well, thank you, Jimmy. If I get to the point where it matters, I'll keep in mind what you've said."

"Besides, I'm referrin you a big case. A good 'un." And Jimmy proceeded to describe a business dispute where the defendant-to-be had delivered obviously nonconforming safety equipment, which had caused injuries already and had had to be expensively replaced. It did sound like "a good 'un." And Jimmy wanted to refer it to Robert?

"Well, Jimmy, send it over. We'll handle it as professionally as anyone. And I'll keep your advice in mind about William Grant."

"Well, but see, I need something from you, Herrick. I'd have to have your assurance, if I refer this case, that you won't sue my good client, the Blackminster Construction Company. That you won't represent William Grant against Blackminster."

The intercom buzzed. "Hold on, Jimmy."

Robert had never gotten used to handling two lines at once. The person he was listening to deserved all his attention. But now, Donna deCarlo said, "It's your wife. She says it's important."

7

Jimmy Coleman was still on the line, he thought to himself. But now, Maria was calling, and it sounded like an emergency.

With a puzzled face, he lifted the receiver. It was likely not an emergency, but instead something she'd found at Saks or Nordstrom and wanted to find out whether he'd like it, but just as likely, it could be a matter of life and death. He didn't know, and he had to answer. And so Maria Melendez's voice came bouncing, as only her voice could, over the line.

"Robert, there's somebody on the other line, calling us from the opera. They want us to know that if we get six operas instead of two, it costs only as much as three. But that special is going away after today."

Robert's wife Maria was unusual. One of a kind. A red-headed Cuban, who had floated up to the Florida shore at age twelve, after her father had bribed his way out of Castro's jails. She laughed a lot, just as she was doing now. "Six operas, Robert!"

Six operas was too many, he said to himself. But he thought fast, with the other line hanging on. With Jimmy Coleman waiting. "Okay, Maria, go ahead. Six operas." He could always give some of these opera tickets away and deduct the cost as a business expense. Maybe.

"Okay! So I should pay for six operas, you think?"

"I . . . guess so."

"Robert! Thank you. But . . . I fooled you! It's not really for the opera. It's for the cost of a Gucci purse. I'm at the Gucci store, and the one I want is on sale, or rather, since Gucci pretends that they don't really have sales—no Gucci sales, ever, they say—it's being sold on

31

some kind of special deal. And I've got to buy it today. And the cost is just the difference between two operas and six."

Maria had an unusual history, and it showed in her sense of humor. After growing up in a bungalow just north of Miami, in Hialeah, she had become a Las Vegas showgirl. "We were a family thing," she always told Robert, when he teased her. "No, it was just a show, silly." But there she was in the newspaper picture, with blue tights, a blue almost-nonexistent skirt, blue feathers, pale Hispanic skin, a beautiful smile, and red hair.

After Las Vegas, she'd gone to law school, and now she was an assistant district attorney. The newspaper picture had a caption: "The Showgirl Who Turned Prosecutor."

Robert groaned. ". . . Gucci purse . . . difference in cost . . . two operas instead of six . . . ."

"That's right, my darling. You're getting a good deal, and it's an amount you agreed was okay."

Maria had an unusual job in the District Attorney's office. When a convict got sentenced to death for a horrific murder, and the never-ending loops of appeals-and-habeas-corpuses-and-stay-applications began, it was her job to pursue the execution of the sentence. It required judgment in unknown and unknowable situations. Sometimes the right thing was to agree with the defense lawyer and settle for a life sentence instead. At other times, it was her job to fight against all kinds of unfounded accusations of impropriety, false allegations of false testimony, and just plain fraudulent claims, to the distant end.

Everyone called Maria by a colorful title: "The DA's Official Killer."

"Okay," Robert said finally. "But . . . what am I saying okay to? . . . Two operas instead of six . . . no, it's not that . . . instead, it's . . . a Gucci purse, and I guess it gets its attractiveness from having the name Gucci stamped on it somewhere. Certainly not from the purse itself, right? . . . ."

He had to laugh at that. And at his own confusion.

But then he cringed. "I feel sometimes like I'm everybody's Daddy in a huge extended family. And I'm the one who always has to think about what things cost. Like now."

It wasn't that she had to ask his permission. If he'd told her that, she'd have told him otherwise, pretty clearly. Instead, it was a matter of his role, which was to consider finances, and hers, which was to keep him from being way too serious and to introduce some spontaneity.

"And also, you have to think about the value of the things we buy," she said. "Like now. And what or who you buy them for." She laughed. "And I'm worth it."

He laughed too. She had won this one. "Okay, baby. Okay. I surrender. Go ahead."

* * *

He looked out the window at the place where the mist of faraway green mingled with blue sky. He thought about meeting Maria Melendez, six years ago.

It had been at a Bar Association meeting, or actually, a cocktail party in an elegant bar. He had said to her, "Hi. Who are you?" And ever since, she had kidded him about his "famous pickup line" and mimicked his voice: "Hi. Who are you?" And she always added, "I guess I must have looked good that day. Or at least, maybe I looked like a girl with loose morals, given the way you think, my darling."

And now, he felt a funny feeling. He loved Maria, but there was the tug of a more distant past. And he reached out toward the gold-framed photograph of his first wife, Patricia, who had died of ovarian cancer. He stretched his hand toward Patricia's picture the way he always did, involuntarily, when he felt something strange around him.

And then, he realized: Jimmy Coleman's still on the line! I almost forgot.

He picked up the receiver. "Jimmy? Sorry about that. My wife."

Jimmy harrumphed. And harrumphed again. When he finally spoke, it was with a croaking voice full of peevishness, the kind that a self-important person exudes when he's not given the attention he thinks he's due.

"I'm gonna send you that case," Jimmy's voice grated. "And it's a good 'un, but I've got to have your assurance that you won't sue my good client, the Blackminster Construction people. My very good client. I'm sure you understand."

"Well . . . I understand what you're saying. But Jimmy, I'm sorry. I've never promised not to represent this person or that person because of something like what you're promising. And I can't start now."

There was another harrumpf, but this time much louder. Followed by Jimmy Coleman's bellow. "If you take on that William Grant case and sue Blackminster Construction Company, you're gonna be sorry as hell. You'll never hear the end of your own client's negligence! You'll feel that contributory fault of William Grant 'till it pushes your head right up your hind end. Right up your ass!"

"Well, thanks for letting me know."

And Jimmy harrumpfed several more times, then severed the connection with a bang.

Robert found himself staring, once again, at the blue-gray tangle of the horizon. And reaching for Patricia's picture. Thinking. And he mumbled again, to himself this time: "It's true. Nothing's ever easy."

* * *

He left as soon as he had briefed Tom Kennedy about the conversation with Jimmy.

Tom just laughed and said, "That's Jimmy Coleman."

"Yep. And now I'm going to get suited up to play baseball."

"Are you in good enough shape for baseball? After Jimmy gave you all kinds of hell and shook you up?"

This time, Robert laughed. "He can do that to me, sometimes. But that's why I need to play ball. It keeps me sane."

* * *

His team was the Cardinals. He was a relief pitcher tonight. His catcher, Mike Gutierrez, kidded him: "Relief means that you get to sit when the game starts, Robert, and that's the kind of relief you need."

"You got that right." Again, he thought to himself: This is what keeps me sane.

The starter pitched for three innings. This wasn't softball, but baseball. With spikes, sliders, and steals. Three innings is about average for amateur pitchers who have to work at day jobs before they play ball. These players were construction workers, delivery guys, policemen, firemen, with an occasional manager of a grocery store thrown in. And on this team, one lawyer, whom everybody appreciated but everybody hoo-rawed—kidded—for his profession.

"Robert," the manager, who was also the team manager, said to him. "You got the next inning. You ready? You got some tricky lawyer stuff to get 'em out with?"

He said what a pitcher always says. "You bet."

"We got a tight game here. Five to three. We're ahead, but don't blow it."

The first batter squared around to bunt. He was bunting for a base hit. Robert caught it in time and threw one of the kinds of pitches that are effective against a bunt: within the strike zone, but high and inside.

But the batter didn't really intend to bunt. He pulled his hands back and ripped that inside ball to left field, just inside the line. Suddenly, Robert had a man on second base with no one out.

He got the next guy out. And the next one after that. But he grooved a fast ball by accident to the next batter, who hit a single through the hole between third base and shortstop. And he gave up a run, because the man on second base was faster than average in the senior league. Of course, you're faster than average in this league if you can run at all.

After he got the next guy out, he walked to the bench with his head high and a big smile. Even if you've done a terrible job, it helps, as a pitcher, to look like a winner.

Gutierrez chuckled at him. "Guy fooled you with that fake bunt."

"He did." Robert laughed too. This wasn't the World Series, and World-Series-seriousness wasn't called for in the senior league.

"Some guys are just gonna pull tricks instead of doing it the usual way," Gutierrez went on. "All you gotta do is watch 'em and you know how to beat them."

Robert was startled for a moment. He thought, That's a piece of wisdom I ought to take away with me.

The same thought applied to lawyers. Gutierrez was talking baseball, but what he was saying fit Jimmy Coleman too. "Some guys pull tricks instead of doing it the usual way. Watch them and you know how you to beat them."

Yes. That's Jimmy Coleman, he said to himself.

"I never play a game of baseball without learning something about the law," he said out loud. "You're right, Gutierrez."

"What you mean is, it teaches you how to be a sneaky lawyer. And a more crooked mouthpiece."

Robert had to laugh, but he filed Gutierrez's theory, about guys who play tricks, away in his mind.

8

While Robert and Tom put the final touches into the suit papers for William Grant, there was the usual kind of activity in the district clerk's office. New lawsuits were filed by internet. Today was a normal day for electronic filing, and the docket clerk was busy.

This particular docket clerk knew he was lucky. He'd been out of prison now for two years after being convicted of aggravated robbery, and he'd managed to keep his life mostly straight. Every day, he remembered that moment so many months ago, when he'd left the unfriendly fencing and wire of the Jester Unit of the State Department of Corrections, and every day, he felt again the fear that had washed over him at that moment.

So, they said that parole was supposed to give you a feeling of sunshine, fresh air, and freedom? Not for me, he thought.

All he had felt was an overwhelming dread. For eight years the world had been changing while he was inside, and for all of that time, he hadn't kept up. He owned nothing, and he couldn't rely on the institution any longer because now, he was out. It was his responsibility to survive, alone.

The docket clerk shivered, now, as he printed the court assignments, thinking about that day two years ago, when he had waited at the bus station. The printer spun out another page. In an earlier time, the designation of which judge would preside over which suit had been done by a rotating system that gave each lawsuit to a court in an particular order, so that the assignments were random—or appeared random. Which judge you got depended on exactly when your lawsuit hit the system and which lawsuits were before you. Now, it was a more modern system. The computer was programmed to generate a random number, which was part of an unknown function, that did the assigning of each lawsuit to a judge.

The printer had spit out the assignments, now, for dozens of lawsuits. Hundreds of people's hopes, dreams, and fears. And the clerk's thoughts drifted back, again, to that day of his release, when the white prison van had delivered him to the bus station. He had carried a bag containing a month's supply of medication. He also had a certificate, earned by completing a junior college education behind bars, announcing to the world that he had received an Associate of Arts degree. His pocket was wadded with a hundred dollars, given to him personally by the warden, in crisp bills. That was the nest egg that this state gave to each departing convict, the stake with which he was to make his way in a hostile world. And, of course, he held a bus ticket that would take him to the big city.

Now, the clerk jerked his attention back to the present. The next step was to send the news to lawyers across the city and throughout the state, telling each one which judge he or she had drawn through the random assignment system. This step was mostly automated too, but he had to verify the documents and stuff the envelopes. Some old-fashioned methods still remained, when the cost of automation was more than the cost of manual operation.

The docket clerk shivered again and worried about the latest threat to his freedom. The latest threat to his life. He had been greeted by a guardian angel soon after his release, a big-shot lawyer named Jimmy Coleman. This man had seemed to care about him when no one else had. The wonderful Mr. Coleman had found him a place to stay and gotten him his job at the clerk's office.

But several months later, there was a catch. As soon as he'd worked up to a position of responsibility in this new job, Mr. Coleman had begun to call on the clerk to perform shady favors. Under-the-table dirty tricks. The clerk found himself creating ways to cut corners for Mr. Coleman: ways to discover slight advantages that could make big differences in lawsuits. For example, the clerk had engineered a rearrangement of the order of trials so that one of Mr. Coleman's lawsuits would be heard earlier than it should have been scheduled.

And then, he had found a way to put an opponent's case on the dismissal docket before its time.

The clerk had been afraid to say No to this powerful Mr. Coleman, but finally he had spoken up. The lawyer had answered, in his rasping voice, "Finish out this year, helping me when I need it, and then we're even." But the clerk worried constantly. All day long, every day, he worried. It was a matter of time until he got caught.

* * *

Later that same day, across town, Jimmy Coleman opened the glass doors beside the big gold letters that said "Booker & Bayne." He surveyed the neat secretarial bays that stretched from one end of the building to the other. All made of white birch, from a single stand of trees in Vermont, all closely matching. As he marched across the heavy tan carpet, he heard the sounds of Booker and Bayne lawyers— working, cajoling, negotiating, soothing, threatening.

"It's easy." That came from behind the door of Cory Gossage, the merger-and-acquisitions lawyer. "You just never deal with the guy again. Yes, I know it will set him back a fur piece. No, don't tell him why. Don't. Nothing you can say will help, and it can only hurt you."

Jimmy smiled. He enjoyed the close-in betrayals that came from that kind of corporate boardroom practice. As he often did when he entered this place, he thought back to Colonel Henry Anderson Booker.

Booker and Bayne had been founded in the 1800's by Colonel Booker. The Colonel had virtually built the city. He had obtained approval for its first set of bonds, pushed through the street plat for River Oaks, and obtained financing for the ship channel. He wore red suspenders and kept a spittoon in his office. The Colonel's motto was, "Find out what the client wants and get it done."

And he always asked, "Is it fair?" But then he found a way to do what the client wanted, fair or not.

By now, Booker and Bayne had hundreds of lawyers all over the world. In Washington, New York, Frankfort, London, Beijing, and points between. They represented The Spinelli Corporation, Kaminsky Interests, Dashiell Motor Company, and others of the Fortune 500. The Colonel was long gone—he had long since found his place in that

Great Courtroom in the Sky from which there is no appeal—but Booker and Bayne continued to grow, and grow, and grow.

It was often said that if any living lawyer represented the spirit of Colonel Henry Anderson Booker, it was Jimmy Coleman.

Now, as Jimmy walked past the office of Talmadge Litton, the real estate lawyer, he heard, "Well, what we want is to make a deal with you. My client can give up that ninety-six acres to get it done. It's blood out of his hide, but he wants to make a deal with you."

Jimmy laughed out loud. If Talmadge Litton was giving them up, he was pretty sure that the ninety-six acres were worthless to the client.

Finally, he found his way to his office. Lisa, his secretary, jumped up to hug him. People said that Jimmy liked Lisa because she was nearly six feet tall, and it was true, because it was well known that Jimmy liked tall women, taller than he was. But Lisa also could sort out Jimmy's clients and calls, get him in touch with whichever far-traveling associate he wanted, and keep her head through Jimmy's under-the-table deals.

"Jennifer's here," Lisa said. Jennifer Lowenstein was his favorite associate.

Jimmy walked into the huge corner office. "Hi," he said to Jennifer, who was sitting almost at attention. "We've got work to do."

"Good."

"Jennifer, let's think who our most reliable judge is these days." Jimmy Coleman sat down in the heavy chair next to the priceless Italian intarsiato chest with blond wood and brown, green, and red vines. The desk in front of him was made to match, with the same inlays, and so were the desk chairs. "We're going to need our best judge, the one who's most favorable to us, in this lawsuit that Robert Herrick's going to throw at us."

"I listened to your voice mail three times, Jimmy. I understand your thinking."

"Judge Patman Greystone isn't a mental giant. Or a Rhodes scholar. But I think Judge Greystone is the one we want. We've given plenty to his re-election campaigns. And he was a dee-fense lawyer for insurance companies before he got to be a judge."

"Well, Robert Herrick's given to him too, of course."

"But we've given more. And besides, Patman Greystone owes me one."

"Of course."

Jimmy Coleman smiled his dirty smile. "Good old Patman Greystone," he croaked. "Here we come."

* * *

The docket clerk lifted the receiver. "It's a lawyer who says he wants to look at a file in the Karanofsky case, and he asked for you."

The clerk shivered. This was what Jimmy Coleman had arranged to say when calling. It kept him one loop away from the action when he wanted a favor.

"Hello . . . Mister Coleman."

And Jimmy greeted him warmly.

Jimmy started with, "I need a slight favor. Just a little one." Jimmy always started out that way, the clerk thought, before asking him to do something that could get him fired or sent back to prison.

"But it's impossible," the docket clerk said with a voice full of disbelief, when Jimmy told him what he wanted.

"I'm sure you'll find a way." Jimmy's words grated in his mouth, but he made them sound soothing. "Remember: it's Greystone. That's Judge Patman Greystone."

9

Two additional men had been injured along with William Grant in the crane hook accident. They would need legal representation too. Right now, the lawyer whose clients they eventually would become was across town. He wasn't thinking about cranes, hooks, courts, or for that matter, anything to do with the law. To be precise, he was at the dog track. Betting on the dogs.

The mechanical rabbit flashed along the track. Behind it, a half dozen greyhounds churned with blurred legs, trying to do the impossible: to catch the prize. But it always eluded them. As quickly as the eye could see, the rabbit crossed the finish line, with the dogs just a few feet behind.

A metaphor, perhaps, for too many fruitless pursuits in life.

The lawyer, whose name was Sammy Stubarsky, jumped and pumped his fist in the air. "Go, Blue Norther! Go, Blue Norther! You're the dog I got, and now . . . you've . . . WON!"

"It's about time," laughed his bearded buddy, sitting beside him. "You already lost four other races today."

"Yeah, but this was the one I knew for sure was a winner. And so, this one more than covers all the other ones."

"What? You knew which one was gonna win, and you didn't give it to me?" The beard showed mock disapproval.

"Nope. You didn't deserve it. Now, let's get a bet down for this next race."

His iPhone rang. "It's the office," Sammy announced. "She knows not to call unless there's money on the other end of the line." He spoke into the phone. "Sheila? Hello?"

"Where are you, Sammy? I can barely hear you over the noise."

"Dog track. Just won. How about that?"

"Great. You know what happens to those greyhounds? Just a couple of years, they race. Then they get euthanized. Ninety-nine percent of them."

"Sheila . . ."

"Or else they get shipped to China, and they arrive in that brutal country half dead, which doesn't matter, because they're going there to get eaten, anyway."

"Sheila, I told you. Don't call me for anything today except if there's money."

"And there is. Maybe."

That got his attention. "Let me go to a place in this stadium where it's not so loud. Up there at the top."

After a pause while he walked to an upper corner of the stadium, he said, "All right, Sheila. Go."

"So, as I was saying, yes, there's money. Maybe."

"Maybe?"

"Well, you know how it is. New client. Hurt. Maybe two new clients. A guy named Bloodhurst or something, on the other line, waiting to talk to you. But as you would say, 'there ain't no money there, till . . . the money's there.'"

"You said . . . Broadhurst? Was it Billy Broadhurst?"

"That sounds right. By the way, I don't think you can represent both of these new guys. Conflict of interest, you know."

"Aw, I never worry too much about that. I went to high school with Billy Broadhurst. Played football together. If he's callin, there's no maybe about it. He's hurt. Put him on."

The sound in the phone changed slightly. Then: "You there?" Sammy blurted. "Billy, you there, my man? Hey, how's it hangin', after all these wasted years?"

After the phone crackled a time or two, Billy's voice came through. "It's bent upward and to the left. That way, you know it's me."

"Yeah. Old Crooked Dick. I been thinkin 'bout you. About how we lost the quarter finals 'cause of you."

"Cause of you there, flyin Tom. If you hadna missed that block . . . ."

"Naw. You got it wrong. But . . . . Say, Billy. You ever heard from Cochise?"

"Good old Cochenase, he's still strummin along. Doesn't answer to Cochise any more."

"Too bad."

Billy Broadhurst's voice changed. "Sammy, I called because . . . . Well, I need help."

"Why? What's up, Broadhurst, my man? You can tell your football buddy. Didja get the pastor's wife pregnant? Didja abscond with government funds? Or didja spit on a preacher, or worse, didja diddle some sorta nun like Mother Teresa?"

"None of the above. I've got a bad, bad broken arm. Doc said it's probably gonna hafta be fused, whatever that means. I won't ever be able to lift anything. Or go duck hunting, cause I can't shoot. I'm alive, but I won't be doin very much that's fun anymore."

"Not even jackin off, I guess."

"I got two arms, Sammy. It's just one arm that's hurt."

"Okay. Got it. I'm serious, now. How'd it happen?"

"Construction site. Crane turned around and hook got dropped. One guy is barely alive, because it split him in the gut like a can opener cuts a tuna box. Then, a half second more, and the hook hit me. Then it hit another guy. And I'm callin you for both of us, actually. People told me, get a lawyer, and Sammy, you're the only lawyer I know."

Sammy stopped listening for a moment. Billy Broadhurst kept describing the accident, but Sammy was already counting the money in his head. It sounded like a good case of liability. And a solvent defendant, probably, although you never knew with construction companies. Still, you could sue everybody in sight and probably hit a target or two. But . . . it was only a broken arm. Not like paraplegic injuries, not nearly as lucrative. Still, this arm sounded broken real good. Maybe, there's money.

Sheila was right. Maybe, there's money.

"Say, Billy. What's the chances of you gettin that other guy to me? The one who's got the split-open gut?" Sammy visualized the negotiations with the crane operator on that case. A really serious case. "Billy, I'll represent you, but I'd also like to represent that guy who got his innards drilled."

"No. I talked to him. He's already got a lawyer."

"Well, let me know if anything breaks there."

"Okay. But for now, I can bring along the third guy. He's my friend, and he's really hurt too, outta the same accident." Billy Broadhurst sounded ashamed that he hadn't steered all three victims, including the guy who was hurt worst, to his buddy Sammy.

"Tomorra, Billy. We'll set it all up. I'm in the office tomorra."

"Say, Sammy. Where you at, right now? I hear a lot of noise."

"At the courthouse." Sammy told his practiced lie. "In the hall, between courtrooms. Someone musta won a big verdict, just like you're gonna win, Billy, and I can hear 'em celebrating, big time."

"All right." Billy was quiet. "Say, Sammy, one other question. Somebody told me that we two might need to have two different lawyers. Two different lawyers, that is, for me and my friend. They said, it's a potential conflict of interest. I want you to represent me, but you may need to get some other lawyer to represent the third guy."

"There's no conflict that I can see." Sammy Stubarsky's voice was flat and confident. "Both of you want the same thing, which is to collect big money and to see each other collect big money. And yes, you're gonna collect big money. See you tomorra. Call back and talk to Sheila about what time tomorra."

When Sammy cut the connection, he was disappointed to see that he had missed two races. Two races, completed while he was on the phone! "And the dog I woulda picked in the race that's happenin now," he said to himself, "is gonna win." A feeling of loss washed over him.

* * *

Robert Herrick was happily unaware of Sammy Stubarsky and the dog track. And as he arrived home, he felt almost normal, not so weighted down, at least momentarily, by William Grant's injuries.

"Maria?" he called, as he walked into the back of the house.

"I'm in the living room, my love." Which was an unusual thing for her to say, and she said it in an unusual voice. In fact, she sounded as though she wanted to laugh, a kind of musical, dramatic voice.

He walked to the front of the house. She was sitting in an arm-chair, looking like the queen of a mideastern empire, except that she was wearing striped multicolored heels and a white T-shirt, which was too big and borrowed from him.

And nothing else.

She jumped and ran to him and put her arms around his neck to kiss him.

"So . . . what did you have in mind?" he asked, and they both laughed.

They stood there for a while, with him holding her and her arms around his neck, kissing each other, lightly and then deeper, then deeper. He felt her hands behind his neck, pulling him, reaching, and rubbing down his back.

He reached under her shirt—or his shirt—and cupped her breasts. He felt her nipples, hard and erect. He felt himself, growing, and erect, too. Her dusky red hair, Hispanic hair, hung down lower than he would have expected. Their lips interlocked, clumsily but almost intentionally, open.

She bent down and pulled his belt. She made him sit and took off one shoe and then the other.

Somehow, she had the T-shirt off, although he wasn't aware of her having taken it off. She still had the colorful shoes.

Now she made him stand and knelt herself. She licked, light then harder, and she ran her tongue from base to tip. Now, he was beyond erect. Way beyond, and feeling almost lightheaded, but full of purpose.

Suddenly, he bent and picked her up, with his hands beneath her arms, and with her feet off the floor. He held her that way for an instant. She was wearing Chanel number 19 and smelled like a woman.

Gently, or not so gently, he rolled her onto her back and onto one of the tan leather couches. Her legs were long and pale and perfect, her body taut and her breasts wide and moving, with reddened nipples. He kissed them, open-mouthed, and tasted her moisture, light and salty.

Her knees were bent. He felt her wetness as he pulled himself between them as he moved. And then they moved together. "We need to get some wider furniture!" she laughed. But however much that issue might matter at another time, it didn't matter now.

They rolled over, and she straddled above him, posting and almost bouncing, slower and then more urgently. Her skin was luminous, and she seemed to glisten, to shine. He could see her climbing, climbing, climbing, until she began with shrill little cries, then a louder, sustained, almost pleading noise, until she slowed. He shuddered, then, as he gave himself up to her.

They lay there for a moment, still. Not speaking. Then she edged, finally, to his side. He sat up to kiss her.

"I guess this is a kind of trial preparation," she said. She said it again, in a dramatic way, "trial preparation," just for fun. And she laughed. She laughed a lot, he thought to himself, sometimes at odd moments, and this time he laughed with her.

10

ello, Robert? It's Sammy Stubarsky."

Robert Herrick recognized the name only by reputation. But what he knew of Sammy Stubarsky's reputation made his forehead wrinkle. Still, you never know, and so he forced himself to answer pleasantly. "Hello, Sammy. What can I do for you?"

The sky outside was misty and wet. Drops of rain clung to the greenhouse-style windows. Robert sat at the big mahogany desk, looking out at the weather, and then at the huge oriental carpet below him.

"As of a few days ago, I represent Billy Broadhurst." Sammy Stubarsky's voice ballooned with self-importance. "You know, the injuries that came out of the crane hook. Same thing that hurt your guy . . . ah . . . what's his name? . . . William Grant. Your client."

"Oh. Okay."

"So, my client, Billy Broadhurst, is the second guy who got hurt. And I also represent the third guy too. That guy who got his face all messed up, and it's still messed up."

"Oh. Okay." Robert wondered, "How can Sammy do that? There'll be a conflict of interest." But he kept the thought to himself. Maybe this Mr. Stubarsky had made all the proper disclosures.

"So, anyway, Robert, we're gonna be partners in this case. One for all and all for one, you know."

"Oh. Okay."

"And I'm just callin to touch base. You got the big enchilada, Robert. You got the guy who's hurt worst. And he's hurt bad, I hear. You gonna set the tone. When you gonna file suit?"

"I don't know. I'm going to contact the other side, first. Jimmy Coleman. That's who represents the defendants. I'm going to contact him first and see whether we can come to an agreement without filing suit. And I've got to find out which defendants to sue if I need to. What the right names are."

"I don't see a problem with that. The names are on the side of their equipment. We can sue everybody with those names."

"Well, yes, I suppose. But if you do that, you run the risk that you sue a bunch of people who have absolutely nothing to do with it. And the judge can sanction you. The judge can make you pay a big fine and pay these innocent people's attorney's fees. Not to mention, you end up oppressing a lot of people who haven't done anything wrong."

"I guess." Sammy Stubarsky's voice was toneless.

"Anyway, I appreciate the call. By the way, where are you, Sammy? I hear a lot of noise. Must be a restaurant or a stadium or something like that."

"Wrong. I'm at the courthouse. Between hearings. You know how it is, in the hallways here. Lots of signs, saying *Quiet: Court in Session,* but nobody pays any attention to the signs, and there's a big crowd outside the courtroom next door for some reason."

"Oh. Okay."

"Anyway, Robert, let me know what you're planning to do about this crane-hook case, okay? We'll coordinate everything. My guys' injuries are less, but they're still good-money injuries, and I'll follow your lead."

"Oh. Okay. Sure, Sammy. It's a deal."

* * *

"What was that all about, Sammy?" The barista was curious.

"Just business." Sammy's voice sounded bored.

"You want another 'un? Another stiffo?"

"Thanks, Mary. A little less branch water and sub-stantially more Bourbon this time. I gotta make another business call in a minute, and it's important, so you know how it is. I need ta' be sharp."

Mary-the-barista giggled at that, because Sammy was already sailing up a whiskey creek. And Sammy laughed with his full throat.

"Don't you ever go to your office, Sammy? I mean, I like having you here, but I wonder how you get it all done. I'm just curious, about how you practice law when you're here all the time."

Mary's hair had about as many colors as a sunset sky on a cloudy day, and she featured three nose rings. Her most visible characteristic, though, was a tattoo of a rattlesnake on both of her arms, with the tail crawling through bushes on one side and the head ending up beside cactus on the other.

"Practicin law? It's mostly thinkin, Mary. And I do some of my best thinkin, after I been drinkin."

"Oh. Okay." She giggled again.

"And now." Sammy stretched and yawned. "Now, I gotta make the next call. Mary, you're in luck. You're about to see law practice in action."

* * *

Jimmy Coleman sat at the flowery desk in front of his priceless Italian chest, which held his golf trophies and first edition books. The windows in his corner office looked to the south, where cars that seemed like ants crawled along the Pierce Elevated Freeway. When he finally spoke, his voice sounded like hailstones in a canebrake.

"Well, Jennifer, we've got Robert Herrick against us again. The accident with the crane hook, you know. Herrick represents this William Grant. The one who's hurt worst. We've been expecting a claim, and we'll fight like Islamic terrorists, because these are good clients we're defending against Herrick."

Jennifer Lowenstein sat across from Jimmy, at one of the ornate desk chairs, which were decorated with the same green-and-brown-and-red inlaid flowers as the chest and desk. She knew what Jimmy's words really meant. Saying that the Blackminster Construction folks were "good clients" didn't indicate that these corporate bullies were civic-minded or even ethical citizens. It mean that they paid millions to Booker and Bayne every year, year after year, without ever questioning the bill, and they expected Booker and Bayne to follow the credo that Colonel Booker had laid down ages ago. "Find out what the client wants, and do whatever it takes."

"So," Jimmy grated, "you know what we're gonna do."

"Contributory negligence." Jennifer smiled. "We'll try these plaintiffs. They're not hurt nearly as badly as they say, and they caused it, themselves. We'll make the issues expand until most of the things that were done wrong were done by the so-called victims."

"Exactly. Reason it works . . . . Well, it's an odd twist of psychology. Guy named Professor Leon Festinger, he named it, years ago. *Cognitive dissonance* is the technical term, in psychology. And it's a simple idea, startlingly simple."

Jimmy smiled like a visting Professor. He was a wonderful teacher, Jennifer thought, no matter what people said about him.

"The psychological theory of cognitive dissonance," Jimmy intoned, "says that people who have contradictory inputs in their heads try to arrange things so that the contradiction—the dissonance—goes away."

Jennifer had heard it before. It was the heart of Jimmy Coleman's blame-the-victim strategy, a method of defending the indefensible. "And so, if people see a terrible accident," she said, "a person who's hurt really badly, in a way that person didn't anticipate . . . ."

". . . And then, the jurors work hard to think of ways that it couldn't happen to them." Jimmy grinned. "The horrible, unexpected injuries they see are one input in the jurors' brains, and their desire to feel safe is another input, and these two thoughts contradict. There's dissonance. They're thinking, this accident can happen to anyone, but I want to believe it can't happen to me. So people want to think of a way to believe, *this accident can't happen to me; it happened to that plaintiff because he was sloppy.* He did something wrong, something I wouldn't do. And almost always, they do manage to think up a way to believe that it wouldn't ever, ever happen to them."

"And if we tell them about a dozen warnings that the plaintiff ignored, a whole bunch of red flags that anyone should have seen, or in other words, a dozen ways that the plaintiff was contributorily negligent . . . ."

Jimmy finished the thought. ". . . They're all too ready to believe it. And that's how we win a lot of big cases. Try the plaintiff. Blame the victim."

"And I've seen it. And it works." Jennifer smiled too.

The intercom buzzed. "Jimmy, it's a lawyer who says it's about the crane-hook accident. A lawyer named Sammy Stubarsky."

"Stay here, Jennifer." Jimmy switched on the speaker. "Hello? Mr. . . . ah . . . Stubarsky?"

"Hello, Mr. Coleman. Sammy Stubarsky here. I represent two guys injured out of that crane-hook accident." His voice boomed with pride. "I don't represent the guy who was cut in the gut—Robert Herrick's got that guy, unfortunately—but I represent the two other guys who were hurt in that accident, and they've got serious cases too."

"I understand your position." Jimmy sounded like a wire brush rubbing on a chain saw. "By the way, you're on speakerphone, and my associate Jennifer Lowenstein is listening too, because she's working on this case with me."

"That's fine. Mr. Coleman, I know your reputation as a superb defense lawyer. I know that you'll represent these crane people as well as anyone ever would. But as you can see, your clients have a lot of—well—what we lawyers call *exposure*."

"I understand your position on that too, Mr. Stubarsky. Expo-o-o-sure, you say. So, assuming you think our good clients, the crane-and-hook people, have some expo-o-o-sure, what's your proposal to do about it?" Jimmy rasped out the word expo-o-o-sure the way a Shakespearean actor might.

Jennifer knew what that meant, too. *Expo-o-o-sure* was a way of saying that Booker and Bayne's client was guilty. In fact, guilty as sin. If the client was only sort of guilty, the message would be simpler, using words like *po-o-o-tential exposure,* or just *trouble,* or even *manageable trouble.* If Jimmy was willing to assume that his clients had expo-o-o-sure, even for the sake of argument, that meant that they'd done something really bad. Really antisocial.

"Well, here's my pitch," Sammy Stubarsky said slowly. "I'll go along with you throughout this case. And you can pin the blame on Robert Herrick's client. And I'll go along with that line. Herrick's client, William Grant, he's the one who positioned all three guys where they were likely to get hurt, and he was the reason everybody was in front of the hook. And Mr. Coleman, you can make sure that my guys get a bundle of money in the end. That way, you'll dodge the real bullet, which is the guy who got his intestines ripped out, and you'll pay a chunk to me, but a lot less than Herrick's going to want."

Sammy seemed to snicker. "Only, here's the catch. We never make an agreement about any of this. No agreements. No deals. This conversation never happened. And we're just sailing along, pursuing this lawsuit, and that's what we'll continue doing. No deals."

Jimmy's eyes grew wide. And bright. "You are a lawyer after my own heart, Mr. Stubarsky. No deals. No deals. But I think I get it. I think I can independently follow those tactics."

"Right."

"No deals, because if we had a deal, an agreement, we'd have to tell the judge about it."

"Right again."

"And we obviously don't want to tell the judge, because the judge would shift things around to take away any advantage a deal could give us."

"Right again. So, we understand our strategy, but there are no deals."

Jimmy was wearing a grin as wide as his face. So was Jennifer. "No deals. But Mr. Stubarsky, I think I understand your strategy."

* * *

Across town, at the bar, Sammy winked at Mary the barista. "And that's how it's done." He nodded to let her know that she had experienced history in the making.

11

The District Attorney's building was a hand-me-down, with offices in odd shapes from past uses, and with carpet that ended in the middles of halls. On the sixth floor, at the entrance to the Appellate Section, sat the secretary for these lawyers. She was known as "The Cussing Mormon."

"Oh, yeah, that's funny as shit, Maria," said Wendy Bachman. "You wanted to get a Gucci purse? Great. And you told your guy you were buying opera tickets instead, so you didn't have to let him know what you were doing? That's dumb as Hell."

"It didn't happen exactly that way." Maria Melendes laughed. "I told him the truth before I bought that purse. And of all the secretaries in this office, Wendy, you are the one with the foulest mouth. And you're also the most judgmental moralist. You've got your big print Bible on your desk right next to the Book of Mormon, but the way you talk, you don't fool me."

"Well, but there's a difference, Maria. All I do is cuss a little bit, and I'm an ordinary citizen. You, Maria, . . . you're an assistant D.A., and you're always pulling pranks. Sometimes they're not illegal, but they're pranks. And some day, you're gonna get your ass in a sling."

"Okay. Okay! I thought the opera ticket thing was just a way to keep peace in the family."

"Well, yeah, and I don't mean to be hard on you. But you love to phone people up and pretend things. And one of these times when you're friggin doin that, you're going to piss off the district attorney from the complaints of some unsuspecting citizen who doesn't know you. And then, you'll get your ass canned."

"Okay. I guess I need to think before I pretend. I got it."

"It's not the Mormon in me, Maria, it's the friend in me, that's talking. Fuckin-A! I don't wanna see you get fired or something."

"I understand. Now, on another subject . . . . About those parole reports I asked you for? I hate to change the subject, but let's get a little business done."

"Yes, I got the file that has your parole reports. You've been adding regularly to it. What's the purpose?"

"I follow the guys and ladies that I sent to the joint. Before I had my current job. I know, I know, I'm probably the only assistant D.A. who does this. It's a way to find out whether what you're doing is working."

"Well, here it is." Wendy handed it over, and she stared when Maria found a particular page. "What's caught your interest?"

"I'm looking at this one guy, who's now in the District Clerk's office. With a great job. As a deputy clerk in the Civil Division, where lawsuits get filed. It surprises me. He must have impressed somebody. He sure didn't impress me. I'm glad he got a job, and I'm glad he seems okay since he got out of prison, but I'll tell you what. I didn't think he'd stay on the straight and narrow. I figured he'd do something and get caught. And get violated. And go right back to the calaboose."

"How would you know, way back then, to predict he'd screw up?"

"Watching people's attitudes when they get paroled, and comparing that to what they've done in the past. Of course, it's not foolproof. That's the whole point. And that's why I watch them, to learn how to guess better. I'd be glad to be wrong in this case, of course."

"You're just waiting for him to fuck up."

Maria laughed. "Well, yes. But I wouldn't have chosen those words. But . . . now . . . I've got to get ready to argue this appeal in the Fifth Circuit next month. That guy who shot all those people in that long string of robberies."

"Okay. I got that file out too. Here. You've got to go get that murdering fucker. He was born for a purpose: to prove why the worst killers should get the death penalty."

* * *

Meanwhile, the deputy clerk who was the subject of this conversation was thinking the same thing. Am I going to be able to stay out of prison?

The telephone had just rung. A call had been transferred to him. "It's someone who wants to see the file in the Baranofsky case. Or maybe, Karanofsky case. Or something."

"It's Mr. Coleman again," the deputy clerk whispered to himself. "That's the signal he uses."

The powerful lawyer's voice came on the line, grating and rasping as usual. "Robert Herrick agreed to tell me when he was filing his suit. And he just called me, just now, to say he's filing it in the next few minutes. Remember, Judge Patman Greystone. It needs to be filed in Patman Greystone's court."

The deputy clerk's skin felt as though invisible insects were swimming through his sweat.

Mr. Coleman's prediction was right. The lawsuit from Robert Herrick, which was called *William Grant v. The Blackminster Corporation,* arrived there less than five minutes later. The deputy clerk felt those imaginary insects scurrying all over his body, and his sweat was gushing.

He had already logged on and typed his password, which was *$$Money.7comeEleven.* He had pulled down the menu. Now, with trembling fingers, he set up the manual bypass. And he reorganized the incoming lawsuits so that William Grant's case went to the 288th District Court. Judge Patman Greystone's court.

He sat back and tried to steady himself. He couldn't stop shaking. But he was unlikely to get caught. Manual overrides were not uncommon.They happened when there were known companion cases following cases already in place, or situations involving known conflicts of interest for judges, or new judges, or retirements, or a dozen other situations.

"Patman Greystone. It's done." He said it out loud. But what he thought to himself was, "Not only is it done, but my bondage to Mr. Coleman has ended."

* * *

Across town, Jimmy sat behind his vine-and-flower-covered desk. "We got it." He raised his fist. His cigar almost fell out of his mouth, his grin was so big.

"Judge Greystone?" Jennifer Lowenstein looked up sharply.

"Yep. It's already on the computer."

"Oh. Okay. Great! Wow!"

"And once again, we've given the client that traditional extra that Booker and Bayne is known for."

"Traditional extra?"

"Remember Colonel Henry Anderson Booker? The Colonel? When I started here, and I was wet behind the ears, the Colonel took a liking to me. And he saw to it that I did things according his motto. Which was, *Find out what the client wants, and find a way to do it.* And now, with Judge Patman Greystone on our side, we'll deliver this one for those good clients at Blackminster Construction Company."

Jennifer laughed. "And the good Judge, Judge Patman Greystone, will indeed be on our side."

Jimmy pumped his arm again. "I can't help it . . . ." He belched a coarse, wet laugh. ". . . I love it. Crooked deals just turn me on."

* * *

Beneath his floor-to ceiling windows, beside the flowers on the big colorful carpet, Robert Herrick peered at the computer screen. "Oh. Great. Greystone."

"What's that?" Tom Kennedy wanted to know.

"Judge Patman Greystone. That's who we've got for William Grant's case, by the luck of the draw. The bad luck of the draw, that is. It's awful luck."

"I don't know about Greystone as well as you do, Robert. But I've certainly heard, he's more defense-minded than middle-of-the-road."

"He's far away from middle of the road. He's a crooked dunce of a judge. This entire case is going to be like jungle warfare in enemy territory, now that we're in Judge Patman Greystone's court."

* * *

Back in Jimmy Coleman's corner office, the gold hardware on the vine-covered Italian chest seemed to glitter a little more brightly than usual.

"Jimmy, why so much effort to get a friendly judge this time?" Jennifer Lowenstein had seen Jimmy pull underhanded tricks before, but this one was unusual.

"Back in the old neighborhood, I learned the Reverse Golden Rule. And that is, 'Do unto others before they do it to you.'"

"How'd you learn that in the old neighborhood?"

"Believe me, Jennifer, you don't want to know."

She was fascinated. If you tell a lawyer "you don't want to know," the lawyer will want to know, even more. "Yes I do!" she said emphatically.

"Well, I don't know about that. I'll tell you just one short and simple story, out of many. The neighborhood I grew up in was gang territory, they called it, and I belonged, just like every other kid I wanted to hang around with. The Deacon's territory butted up against ours, and those Deacons were vicious little bastards. Of course, we were too."

"And?" she asked.

"And there came a day when about a dozen or so Deacons came on our grounds. They just poured across La Cienega Boulevard. A dozen bad guys from another band of bad guys is like an army. Might as well have been an invasion. We had to do something. Our guys spread out around them. And shot them up. Before they did anything. Because they obviously meant to do something. We didn't end up killing anyone, but that was a miracle. I can't see how it happened, that we didn't kill anyone."

He paused, and looked out at the clouds, and then at the cars crawling on the freeways, so many stories below.

"There was a guy we called Crackers, because he was crazy, and it was old Crackers who said it. I mean, Crackers summed it up, about shooting the Deacons. 'It's the Reverse Golden Rule,' Crackers said. *'Do it to others before they do it to you.'* Everybody laughed, because it was funny. Crackers was nuts, but he was pretty intelligent, and he used words well. And also, everybody felt good because we had done a good job, and everybody knew that the more vicious you are, the more your reputation."

Jennifer just said, ". . . Oh."

"But listen, Jennifer. Forget about that silly little story. It's long in the past. But remember this. You gotta anticipate. And if you anticipate, you'll prevent a lot of trouble by doing it to others before they do it to you."

Jimmy laughed. "And that's what we've done, just now, about Robert Herrick's lawsuit."

12

The Methodist Hospital has not just one intensive care unit, but five. The Cardiac ICU is probably the busiest. There, the doctors transplant a heart at the rate of about one a week. But the biggest variety of sick people is in the "Other" ICU. "Other," that is from the other four, with unusual kinds of illnesses and injuries, ranging from exotic strains of pneumonia to newly minted versions of streptococcus.

William Grant was here now, in the "Other" ICU. For the second time. He had arrived by ambulance, with stomach pains severe enough to make him drift into and out of consciousness.

It was apparent that the hook that had torn Willie's abdomen open had somehow created his condition now. But what would have been the immediate cause? And what would the response be, for whatever odd infection or injury was controlling it?

A resident doctor was dictating the answer, to become part of Willie's monster medical chart. "X-ray disclosed an abscess in the pancreatic region," he intoned. "Microincision produced a sample, which was isolated from air by clinical procedures and sent to laboratory in transport medium, maintaining an environment preventing introduction of air. The specimen was cultured in a petri dish, which contained selective agar for internal bacteria.

"Culture showed presence of Bacteriodes fragilis, commingled with Escherichia coli. B. fragilis, of course, is the most common infectant that arrives after intestinal invasion, and E. coli is a common companion. Recommend surgical treatment of the abscess followed by antibiotic therapy."

William Grant's wife had been sleeping in the waiting room just outside the ICU. Hearing the news, and learning that it would not be life-threatening, she said, "Thank God. I thought I had lost him this time. He was hurt as bad, when we came to the hospital, as the hook hurt him in the first place." She had told her son, when he asked, to contact the church and the funeral home.

Grant himself still suffered from the exquisite agony that a gut injury can create, whenever the opiates tamping down his pain tended to disappear from absorption.

Jimmy Coleman heard the news three days later, when Robert Herrick and Associates sent their amended disclosures for the case. "It's nothing," he told Jennifer Lowenstein. "Just routine. But unfortunately, it will pump up the damages we'll have to fight. Herrick will be arguing about phony stuff like pain and suffering, you know."

* * *

Across the state, in the capital city, the Governor shoved back his red hair and pushed away from his big desk. "Okay. So there's this vacancy on the Fourteenth Court of Appeals. Where's the Fourteenth Court of Appeals?"

His judicial aide nodded. "It's in the southeastern part of the state. A bunch of coastal counties."

"How did this vacancy happen? Not any of the judges with a hand in the cookie jar, I hope."

"No." The Governor's aide laughed. "It's the usual reason. One of the Justices on that Court of Appeals, named Bartiromo, resigned. She said she had family commitments. Translation: she has kids in school and is going back into practice to make more money."

"I wish I was making more money."

"Don't we all, Chief. But that's the story."

"So, what do I do about this vacancy on the Fourteenth Court of Appeals?"

"I'd suggest moving Judge Patman Greystone up to the Court of Appeals from the District Court. He's got a lot of supporters. Big-time lawyer named Jimmy Coleman, at Booker and Bayne, started pushing Greystone for the Court of Appeals two years ago."

The Governor frowned. "Jimmy Coleman's a sleazebag."

"Well, but he heads the political contributions from Booker and Bayne. That Booker and Bayne PAC spreads out a lot of big money. And as for Jimmy Coleman, he steered over a hundred thousand to your last campaign."

"Now, look there. Why'd you get me to say bad things about a fine lawyer like Jimmy Coleman?" The Governor laughed. This was easy stuff, appointing judges, and he was having a good time. "Of course Jimmy's not a sleazebag. Why'd you trick me into saying he was?"

The aide laughed too. "Sorry, Governor. Inadvertence on my part."

"All right. Greystone it is. And now, we've got to replace Greystone."

"It's a two-fer, Governor. You can do favors for two groups of donors and constituents. Once for the Court of Appeals, and once for the District Court."

"Good. I like that."

"For right now, the issue will take care of itself. Patman Greystone's cases will be spread out among the existing judges. And meanwhile, we should study the situation about the District Court."

"Oh. I see."

"You really need to appoint a Latino, maybe a woman or a Latina if possible, to this District Court judgeship. And that's a minority, not only in the usual sense, but it's a small percentage of the lawyers, who are Latino. Or Latina. We'll have to interview and vet the possible Latina lawyers to find one to appoint. Carefully. We just have fewer of them in our party."

"All right. It's late in the day anyway. Time to make the Capitol Club and drink some bourbon with the leadership of the legislature."

"I'll notify Greystone to expect your call and get the ball rolling on his new position. He'll be appreciative, and so will Jimmy Coleman."

The Governor laughed. "And Jimmy Coleman's not a sleazebag, of course."

* * *

But Jimmy was not appreciative. Instead, he just sat in front of his priceless Italian chest and shook his head unhappily. "Here we are, Jennifer, victims of our own success."

Jennifer Lowenstein frowned. "Why? What's happened?"

"After busting our rear end to get Patman Greystone as our judge in that William Grant case, where he could have helped us defend our good client Blackminster, Patman Greystone isn't the judge of that court anymore. And the case has been transferred to Judge Manny Lopez."

"Oh! That's bad. I know how much you wanted Greystone."

"And we got him. At first. But not now, and I'm to blame for my own misfortune. Starting two years ago, I pushed the Governor's office to elevate Greystone to the Court of Appeals. And they did it. I just got a call from the Governor's office. They mentioned my support of Greystone. They expected me to gush with thanks. We succeeded, but what we really did, was that we shot ourselves in the foot."

"Ouch. And Judge Manny Lopez?"

"Well, he's not exactly an enemy. He's a straight-down-the-middle judge. But the problem is, we need all the help we can get in this William Grant case."

"I see. But Jimmy, I guess we'll just have to get in there and win the case the old fashioned way."

Jimmy Coleman smiled, but it was an unpleasant smile. "Yep. That's what we'll do," he croaked.

13

The Court of Appeals for the Fifth Circuit sits in a gray building that looks exactly like what it is: a federal courthouse of last resort. A few disputes, like stalks blown miles from a haystack, make it up to the Supreme Court, from here. But for all but the rarest cases, this Court of Appeals is the final stop. For a death penalty convict, this will be the place where ultimately, the repeated round of appeals and habeas corpus petitions will end.

Maria Melendes had stood, with two dozen other onlookers, when the loud bang! that preceded the judges had echoed from behind the back door. A law clerk had knocked on the door and barked the traditional opening line: "Hear ye, hear ye, hear ye! The United States Court of Appeals for the Fifth Circuit is now in session." Everyone had remained standing while the three judges, two women and a man, each wearing loose black robes, had walked in conspicuous silence to their big chairs behind the long bench. The entire scene was staged to emphasize the majesty of the federal government.

"Be seated," said the judge in the middle, the presiding judge. "We've read your briefs in each of today's cases and are familiar with them, and you should not address matters that we already know." She looked at the docket sheet. "The first case on the docket is *Landers v. Texas*. Speaking for the convict under sentence of death is Mr. Arthur Herrera, appointed by this court to represent Mr. Landers. Speaking for the state government, in response, will be Ms. Maria Melendes."

The judge pushed her glasses and looked down. "Mr. Herrera, please concentrate on telling this court why you think it should overturn the judgment of the District Court, which has upheld Mr.

Landers's sentence. And please do it without referring to your opponent as learned counsel, or the court as this honorable tribunal, or any other linguistic flourishes."

Herrera was a big man, and he lumbered to the podium in a loose gray suit. He fished around with his papers while giving the traditional first line: "May it please the Court . . . ."

"Mr. Herrera," replied the presiding judge. Unnecessary, of course, because everyone knew by now that he was Mr. Herrera, but the judge said it because, again, it was traditional.

"There are many reasons for reversing this unjust judgment, your Honors. I will take the Court's advice and leave most of them to the written brief. But there are two that I would emphasize here. First, the prosecutor at Mr. Landers' trial violated the Fifth Amendment when he told the jury that the evidence of intent to kill was 'uncontradicted.' Second, the jury wasn't told directly enough that they should consider all mitigating evidence, or all of the evidence that weighed *against* a sentence of death."

The defense lawyer held up one finger. "So, the first point. When the only obvious person who could *contradict* particular evidence of guilt is the *defendant* himself, an assistant district attorney cannot properly argue to the jury that the evidence is *uncontradicted*. It becomes an argument by the prosecutor that focuses the jury on the defendant's failure to testify. In this case, Mr. Landers invoked his right against self-incrimination and did not testify. But the prosecutor told the jury at the end of the case that the evidence of intent to kill was 'uncontradicted.'"

The judges listened with silent attention as the defense attorney went on. "The basic case is *Griffin v. California*. There, as the court knows, the Supreme Court held that it is a constitutional violation to suggest guilt based on the defendant's failure to testify. The cases most directly on point, saying that the 'uncontradicted' argument is ground for reversal, are cited in our brief."

Sitting behind Herrera, Maria marvelled, for perhaps the hundredth time, at the saccharine emptiness of appellate arguments in death penalty cases. Whether the defendant was guilty had almost nothing to do with anything. How horrible the murder was—that didn't matter much either. It was all about procedural niceties, arguments as thin and bloodless as taffeta, that formed the foundation for castles in the air.

But Mr. Herrera was doing the job well, making a substantial argument out of what seemed like next to nothing. Maria had answers to both of the defense lawyer's attacks on the conviction, but the outcome depended, as it always did, on the judges' distant and novel points of view. She listened as the defense argument seemed to hammer away against what she thought was the only just outcome.

Suddenly, she found herself thinking about her husband. "I wonder," she said to herself, "how Robert is doing with his difficult case, today. The crane hook case."

But then she jerked herself back to the business at hand. The defense lawyer was explaining why the trial judge's instructions to the jury were just not clear enough.

Finally, the presiding judge intervened firmly. "The light is flashing. Time's up, counsel. You may finish this sentence, but don't put too many ifs or ands or buts into it."

Then, after Mr. Herrera turned and left, the judge said: "Ms. Melendes."

Maria stepped to the podium. As she had learned to do from many arguments, she carried nothing with her but an empty manila folder. On its front, its two insides, and its back were notes about all of her arguments and the names of precedents she might need.

"May it please the Court."

"Ms. Melendes."

* * *

In fact, Robert Herrick was miles away, meeting with William Grant. His client.

"You're still in pain?"

The man sitting in the wheelchair shrugged. "It comes and it goes. Today is a good day. I want your advice. I'm here to learn. You said that the other side is going to take my deposition today. I have no idea what that means. What's a *deposition*?"

"A deposition is nothing other than the other side interviewing you, questioning you, under oath. You'll swear to tell the truth. A court reporter will take down every word. A videotape camera will be watching too. And this is the way that lawyers find out what the witnesses for the other side are going to say. In fact, we—your lawyers—will be taking depositions too, of the other side's witnesses. The witnesses against us."

"So. I have to be sharp." A smile.

Robert smiled too. "That's right. You have to be sharp when your deposition is taken."

"And I have to convince them, the other side, that we're right. It's sort of like a gladiator in the ring."

"Well, no, William. No. You have to be sharp, yes, but no, this isn't necessarily the place where we're going to be winning the case."

"Why not?" A puzzled look.

"Because the other side wants to pick your brain. Their questions will be leading questions. They'll try to get you to slip up. They'll be waiting for you to make a mistake. They want you to run off at the mouth and say all kinds of things. That's what they want you to do, to talk a lot. The worst thing you can do is to try to persuade the other side with a lot of talk and rhetoric."

". . . Oh. Okay . . . . Well, okay. But what do I do, then?"

"First thing, and I want to emphasize this: *Tell the truth.* Some people think it's a game without rules, and they exaggerate or cover up things or even tell a fictional story. Don't, don't, don't do that. *Tell the truth.*"

"Okay. So, I should tell everybody you and I never had this conversation, right?"

"No. No! Tell the truth. You met with your lawyer. It's an old trick, to ask in a deposition, *Did you discuss your testimony with your lawyer?* And if you say no, and it's untrue, that's a disaster. You've got to *tell the truth.* There's nothing wrong with telling everybody that you discussed it with your lawyer. You're expected to."

"Oh. Okay."

"But here's the key. You should answer every question, truthfully, and then *stop.* Don't say more than what's required to answer the question. For example, if you're asked, what kind of car do you drive, the answer is a Chevrolet. Or a Ford. Or whatever it is. Not 'a Chevrolet Malibu with sporting headlights and the extra chrome package and an accelerator pedal that sticks.' Remember, they want you to run off at the mouth. But don't."

"Oh. Okay."

"So, William, you've got the idea. Answer, and be truthful, but then stop. Let's try it. Imagine now that I'm the other lawyer, asking you questions in a deposition. I'm on the other side. I'm the opponent. And my first question is, *William Grant, what kind of car do you drive?* And so, what is your answer?"

The man in the wheelchair understood. He grinned all the way across his face and spoke dramatically. "A *truck!*"

"You've got it."

* * *

Meanwhile, Maria Melendez stood before the three judges of the Court of Appeals. "Ms. Melendes."

She had struggled to keep her thoughts on track and away from her husband's case.

"About Mr. Herrera's first argument, we agree that *Griffin v. California* says the prosecutor can't encourage the jury to take the defendant's silence as evidence of guilt. And we agree with him that some of the cases say an assistant district attorney can't say the evidence is *uncontradicted* if the only witness who could contradict it is the defendant himself. But that's not even close to this case. There were lots of other witnesses. The evidence showed that Lester Landers went into a convenience store and made the clerk lie on the floor. And shot him in the back of the head. But there were five other people in the store whom he also shot, two of whom survived and testified."

She raised a hand slightly. "So, the defendant was *not the only witness.* And all of the witnesses who testified—they described the same conduct committed by the defendant. Their testimony was uncontradicted. It was consistent, in other words. And there were five other robbery-murders by this defendant. All of them involved witnesses who testified to the same horrifying conduct by this defendant: making people lie on the floor and shooting them while they begged and prayed. This isn't a case where the defendant was the only one who could have contradicted anything, and it doesn't involve a violation of *Griffin v. California.*"

She had momentum now. Her shakiness was gone. The rest of her argument was smooth, almost like a conversation, until the presiding judge finally called time.

As she sat down, she knew it would be a long time before this case could be resolved. It would take anywhere from two weeks to two years for the court to write an opinion ordering the conviction affirmed or reversed. And that ruling would only lead to more loops of habeas petitions or appeals. Capital cases, Maria reminded herself, move slowly.

But now, it was time to go back to the office. And she thought, again, "I wonder how Robert is doing."

14

This chair is too damn little." Jimmy Coleman sat down, heavily, and emitted a florescent cough. "Let's get this deposition underway. I got some important stuff to do today."

"Raise your right hand," said the court reporter to William Grant.

The man in the wheelchair swore to tell the truth.

Jimmy Coleman started abruptly. "You're gonna tell the truth, William Grant?"

". . . Ahhh. . . Yes. Yes." The plaintiff was startled. It was an odd first question.

"Well, you haven't so far. In your petition, it says that Billy M. Broadhurst was standing next to you when all of this happened. But his name is Billy R. Broadhurst, isn't it?"

"Ahhh . . . yes, if you say so."

"You didn't tell the truth there, did you, William Grant?"

"Don't answer that," Robert Herrick said quickly to his client. "Mr. Coleman, I object to your harassment of the witness. He's not responsible for the papers drawn by his attorneys. We'll terminate the deposition if you continue that. You can go on to another subject."

But Jimmy had already succeeded. William Grant was now a package of jumbled nerves, and he was ready to be confused, even by simple questions.

"You had your back turned when the hook was coming around, didn't you, William Grant?"

"Ahhh . . . yes."

"And if you hadn't turned your back, you could have seen the hook, and nothing would have happened, right?"

71

"Ahhh . . . I guess so."

"You were contributorily negligent yourself, weren't you?"

"Ahhh . . . I don't know what that means."

"Turning your back was a careless thing, wasn't it?"

"I guess so . . . ."

"All right. That's what contributory negligence means."

"Don't answer that," said Robert Herrick again. "I don't want to terminate this deposition, because we've got to get it done, but Mr. Coleman, you know that's not a question. Confine yourself to asking questions, please."

Jimmy shrugged. His voice sounded like sandpaper on metal. "And William Grant, did you listen when you heard that the crane was coming about, or coming around?"

"Yes."

"You knew what that meant, didn't you?"

". . . Yes."

"Wasn't that another case of your being contributorily negligent, not reacting when you knew the crane was coming around?"

"Ahhh . . . I don't know."

Robert stirred in his seat. It was painful to watch. A lawyer who prepares his client for cross examination is like a parent who prepares a child for a difficult task and then can only sit by helplessly while the boy or girl makes mistake after mistake.

It was like watching his client get beaten up. In this state, the rules of litigation don't allow a lawyer much room to help during a deposition, unless the questions are really harassment. And most of Jimmy Coleman's questions were relevant to the lawsuit. However much they looked like mistreatment of William Grant, Jimmy was entitled to ask these questions. Or at least, most of them.

An hour passed. The court reporter needed a break. The deposition resumed. Another hour. Another break. Another hour, and another break.

Finally, five hours after he had begun to ask questions, Jimmy Coleman was ready to wind up. He had scored dozens of admissions of carelessness from William Grant, which he reminded the plaintiff each time, were the same as dozens of admissions of contributory negligence.

"Mr. Grant, do you think you've understood my questions?"

"Ahhh . . . yes."

"Have I been polite to you?" And Jimmy had been polite during the last hour, while the man in the wheelchair had sagged with weariness and had agreed too easily with his combative opponent's leading questions.

"Yes."

"I got no more questions of *this* witness." Jimmy spat the words out, as if to say, William Grant is a silly plaintiff and this is a groundless lawsuit.

Robert Herrick merely said, "I pass the witness too." He had told William Grant he probably would do this, without asking any questions. It doesn't usually pay to try to repair the damage in a deposition. There's almost always damage, but if a lawyer tries to repair it now, all he does is to interview his client in front of the adversary, tipping his hand and giving more ammunition to the other side.

Jimmy had done what he had set out to do. And there was nothing to do that could fix things, now.

* * *

"I feel like I let you down." William Grant was miserable.

"You did fine. You did absolutely fine." Robert found that he was surprisingly upbeat.

"He got me to say a lot of things I didn't want to say. Even that my pain wasn't that bad."

"He got you to say that it wasn't that bad, *compared to other people with life-threatening injuries*. And that's all right."

"I didn't know what to say. When it comes to pain, it's not measurable. You can't really compare."

"Of course. We'll tell the jury that. In fact, the jurors know that. We've got answers for all of the unfair stuff that Coleman asked you."

"Can he play this video back to the jury? I don't want that, for sure."

"The answer is yes. But William, listen. You did fine. You were solid. You told the truth, and it shows. And Coleman was overbearing and pushy. If he does play it back, which I doubt, the jury will see what a bully he was."

He hoped it was true. But he thought to himself: juries are different every time, and they don't always think the way lawyers would like them to.

15

The G-2 aircraft descended to 20.000 feet. "Welcome to Alaska," said the pilot's voice over the loudspeaker.

Maria Melendes was sitting at the bar in the aft of the aircraft. She held up a glass of champagne. "Here we are. Alaska!" She declared. Green, green land sped by beneath them, with alternating patches of grass and trees. "I never knew that Alaska would be so lush and full of vegetation."

"That's right. The climate around Anchorage is milder than most people would guess," Robert said.

"How many times have you been up here?"

"Three times before this, on William Grant's case. I'm glad I have this airplane."

"But it's old fashioned." She laughed. "Shouldn't you at least have upgraded to a G-4 by now?"

He laughed too. "My job is to watch the money. Evidently, yours is to think about how to spend it. This G-2 is an excellent plane. No reason to get another one."

"You're just a miser." She laughed again.

The pilot's voice came over the speaker. "Everybody check your seat belts. We're descending, now, for real. But watch the scenery. We're now going inland from the Gulf of Alaska." The aircraft banked lightly.

"Now," Robert said, "the sightseeing tour begins. Chuck turned in a flight plan that will let us look at some beautiful water, land, and shoreline."

And with that, the G-2 banked hard to starboard.

"Chuck's turning to take us up Cook Inlet. This is a long body of water that separates the Alaskan mainland from the barrier islands, if you want to call them that. Cook Inlet stretches for miles, and Anchorage, the biggest city in Alaska, is at one end of it. Well, not quite the end."

"Can I have some more champagne?" Maria wanted to know.

"Better do it quickly. Because then you've got to come here and put your seatbelt on."

"Are you the flight attendant?"

"Best substitute on this particular flight, yes."

She buckled herself in, with the champagne flute in her hand.

The sunlight rippled on the water. The waves were tiny, on a calm sea, and Cook Inlet was filled with broad stripes of light and dark. A promontory sped by down below, like a finger of earth shooting out into the water, with forest and grass patches all over it, and with a few houses gleaming in white and silver.

"That's Kustatan, down below." Robert said. "That peninsula. We're almost ready to arrive."

"Good. It's been a long trip." Tom Kennedy was half asleep. Robert's two children, Pepper and Robbie, were soundly sleeping still.

"Yes. It is a long trip, even if you don't stop in Seattle, the way we did."

More water went by below, with green shores on both sides and with odd shapes of land jutting out. alternating between trees and grassland.

"About now, we'll start to go down faster," Robert said, "to descend toward Anchorage."

The flaps went down. The noise of the aircraft changed, and the descent was steeper.

"What's your plan, Robert," Maria wanted to know, "about when you're going to go where, and what to get done?"

"Main thing is, tomorrow Tom and I are going to meet with the emergency doctor who treated William Grant right after the accident. Next day, we take his deposition."

"Okay. I want to go see some glaciers. And maybe some Indians, with feathers and beads and stuff."

The aircraft banked to port and headed toward green earth.

"There's an ice sheet nearby that they call Portage Glacier," Robert said, "over to the west of Anchorage. About an hour away. It's awesome. And shrinking, they think. So take the rent car and the kids and drive down there."

He shook his head. "But there aren't any Indians with feathers around here. I'm sorry. It's a modern city, a real city, whatever wild images you might think up."

"That sounds good for a glacier trip, but it's too bad about the Indians."

Trees and grass and occasional buildings rushed by.

"All right. We're over the land now, because Chuck is bringing us into Ted Stevens Airport. We've been heading basically northeast. He's circling around to head us almost due east, toward the runway."

An odd-shaped piece of earth appeared below.

"See that little chunk of land, up front?" He pointed. "That's Fire Island. A tiny green bump. It's shaped basically like a teardrop that is sort of tilted on its side. Lots of trees."

"Okay. So, why's it called Fire Island instead of Teardrop Island, Mr. Tour Guide?"

"Because they didn't ask me."

The aircraft dipped rapidly, now. With the setting sun behind it, the craft headed into the promontory that is Anchorage, Alaska. The taller buildings of the city loomed before them, in the distance—not tall by, say, Manhattan standards, but substantial buildings, perhaps more substantial than one might expect in Alaska.

A few minutes later, the G-2 glided onto the runway.

* * *

Early the next morning, Robert and Tom walked the short distance from their hotel to the Medical Towers Building. There, on the eleventh floor, they were greeted by Dr. Fahir Hasheen.

"I remember this patient as clear as day," the doctor said. "William Grant. It was a most unusual case, with injuries of this kind."

He led them to a small office and had them sit.

"How did you get to Alaska, Doctor?" Tom asked first.

"I'm a native." The doctor laughed. "Whenever someone comes here from the lower forty-eight, the first question is always, 'Tell me how you got here.'"

"Well, I guess I'm like a tourist here," Tom said and laughed.

"No problem," said the doctor. "But the answer is, I actually came here by being born. I'm Alaskan through and through. I went to Medical School at Emory in Atlanta and did my internship and residency in New York, but I always intended to come back here. My father came from Egypt, though, and I guess that's what you're really asking."

"An Egyptian Alaskan. Sounds like solid American," Tom said.

"And I'm here in Anchorage because I like the tropical weather, of course." The doctor had a sense of humor.

"Doctor," said Robert, "we need to ask some questions about William Grant. Please tell us, in a general way, how this patient presented. What I'm getting at is, what did you see, and what were your impressions?"

"That's a long story, even though it involved getting the man on the operating table, stat, in a few seconds. The external bleeding had been stopped or at least slowed by contact bandages, but the injury was most unusual and most severe. Removing the bandages, I could only imagine that most of the abdominal structures were damaged. His organs were like raw hamburger, or bloody oatmeal."

Doctor Hasheen paused, remembering. "First problem was to clamp the bleeders. And at the same time, establish an IV and begin transfusion and antibiotics. It was a bad injury. One of the complexities was that there were a lot of inclusions, by which I mean debris, and half of it was just plain old dirt. Construction site injury. Those tend to be serious. You see patients in the emergency department who've had abdominal trauma, abdominal rupturing, and other kinds of invasions, but this one, by the length of the wound and its depth, really stood out. The man is lucky to be alive, I'd say."

"He's probably lucky to have had you as his doctor. But anyway, tell us why you think he survived, when I guess not everybody would."

The doctor looked at Robert. "That's right. How did he survive? I think, first of all, that the man was in excellent physical shape for his age."

Robert nodded at Tom, and they both made notes. This would be an important point, if only for the comparison between the much weaker William Grant now and the strong Little Willie back then.

"The man's a fighter," the doctor went on. "We withheld pain medication part of the time, at first, because of the bleeding. He's tough. He lived through it all and worked at it. I mean, he worked at living through it. Some people do and some people don't. Also, I think the safety crew at the job site got him here quickly, and the paramedics did the best that they could. It was all of those things coming together, everything, that made him survive."

Another nod from Robert to Tom, and more notes.

"Doctor, we've already got the medical chart, and we've been over it step by step with the forensic nurses in our office. They're only nurses, even if they're very good. But you're the real doc who did it. We want to go over the medical care that you gave to William Grant in the Emergency Department, step by step. So, okay, you've got him up on the table. What's first?"

"Well, step number one was to stop the bleeding. And at the same time, the scrub nurse established an IV and the anesthesiologist began transfusing him. O positive blood. We didn't know his type and didn't have time to wait to test it. And antibiotics. Then, there was a lot of cleanup. Just picking out foreign matter, piece by piece, swabbing and picking . . . ."

* * *

An hour and a half later, they had Dr. Hasheen's full story, and they had almost finished preparing him to testify.

"Doctor," Robert said, "we don't anticipate asking you to come to the trial to testify. We're going to record your testimony by deposition, on videotape, and play that for the jury. The lawyer on the other side is Jimmy Coleman, and we've prepared you for some of the questions he might ask. He's—well—Mr. Coleman is overly thorough and not always pleasant to deal with. He may give you trouble, or try to. We won't let him be a harasser, but he'll ask pointed, leading questions."

Robert paused, at that. "But the point, now, is that this will be an unusual deposition. You've had your deposition taken before, I'm sure?"

"Unfortunately, yes."

"It happens to most doctors, and it always will, as long as they have to treat injured patients. Not something you'd prefer to spend your time doing."

"For this patient, I'm glad to do it."

"But this deposition will be different, doctor. We will be asking you questions that we will use to prove what happened to William Grant. To play in front of the jury. We cannot ask you what are called 'leading questions.' So, when we're asking something, try to figure out what we're asking and answer completely. The other side can ask you leading questions."

"I'm familiar with those, leading questions. The lawyers try to put words in my mouth, and I can't let them. And so I think I know how to answer those questions."

"All right. Let's leave it there. Thank you, doctor, so much, so much, for your time. And I can tell you, your patient William Grant appreciates it too."

* * *

The next day, the deposition of Dr. Fahir Hasheen lasted five hours.

"That was exhausting," said Tom as they exited the building.

"Mostly because of Jimmy," Robert added.

"We got what we needed. But Jimmy messed it up."

"He thinks that's his job. Unfortunately, we're always going to have opponents."

Tom finished the thought. "And nothing's ever easy."

Maria Melendes lifted their spirits, finally, by showing them a picture of the totem pole she had bought in a big store called "Real Alaska" on the outskirts of town. It would go in a corner of the back yard, she explained.

"And no shipping cost, Robert. That's probably because the cost of the totem pole itself was pretty substantial."

As usual, she made everyone laugh.

16

"O rder in the court." The law clerk announced it with obvious pride in himself. "Everyone rise, please."

Now, the battle had shifted. Back home, at the courthouse.

Judge Manny Lopez climbed to the bench, told everyone to be seated, and set about hearing the thirty-plus motions that were set for this morning.

"And we're number twenty-two," said Tom Kennedy to Robert. "We'll do nothing for a couple of hours."

"Yes. If you want to be a good trial lawyer, what you end up doing is twiddling your thumbs a lot, unfortunately."

"Even if you want to be a bad trial lawyer."

"And the bits of time that you waste are hard to use in another way, even for reading, because they're chopped up and because you have to be listening even if you're just waiting."

And so, they sat and listened. The first case was a motion for summary judgment. In other words, it was a request that the judge terminate the case because the issues were clear enough so that a trial wasn't needed. Judge Lopez listened to the lawyers for three minutes and then announced his ruling. Motion denied. The second motion was by a plaintiff who wanted the defendant to hand over every record that involved another accident with the same kind of machinery. After less than three minutes, the judge ruled. Motion denied.

The third motion was for protection from having to give a deposition. It seemed that the defendant was afraid of the plaintiff because they had once had an argument that had ended in a fistfight, and he wanted to avoid having to answer questions with the plaintiff present. Motion denied. "Give the deposition. I'm sure you'll be safe."

And so on.

Robert and Tom were listening, trying to collect hints about how this particular judge was acting today. "He's in a hurry," said Tom. "Wants to get on to other business, like maybe a jury trial this afternoon."

Robert was more cynical. "Or go home and sack out, maybe."

"And it looks as though he's in a mood to deny everything, if he can."

"Right. We'll have to seize the initiative from Jimmy Coleman and hammer away with our best shot."

And the judge's hearing of motions went on. And on. For the thousandth time, Robert found himself thinking how glad he was, not to be a judge. You have to be patient if you're a judge. You have to listen until it's coming out of your ears. But you have to move things along, hurry things along in fact, or your docket will grow and grow until it is unmanageable. So, you have to make decision after decision, quickly and with only partial information. And making decisions is hard work.

In fact, the strain was already beginning to show on Judge Manny Lopez. "Look how he snapped at that lawyer for being slow to get to the point," Tom said.

"I'll have to be quick, and catch Judge Lopez's interest," Robert agreed.

*   *   *

It was over two hours later when Robert and Tom heard the Judge call their case. "Grant v. The Blackminster Construction Corporation."

Jimmy Coleman waddled down to the courtroom well, right in front of the bench. So did Sammy Stubarsky, and so did Robert and Tom.

"It's a motion by Mr. Herrick for a preferential setting of the trial," said Judge Lopez. "An early setting. On a certain date. Why, gentlemen?"

"Robert Herrick, here for William Grant." He said it as fast as he could. "This case is about my client having his abdomen ripped open, a life-threatening injury, and he has never recovered from it. He's already had one emergency trip by ambulance back to the hospital, and we are holding our breath, expecting it to happen again at any time. We can't know that he will still be alive if his case is tried a year from now. Or two years from now, or three, as the dockets are today."

"I see," The judge didn't sound unsympathetic, but he didn't sound sympathetic either.

"We are begging the court for a preferential trial setting," Robert went on. "An early trial setting, to increase the chances that the plaintiff won't be dead, so he can appear alive to tell the jury what happened to him."

The judge had a fist under his chin and was resting on it, with his elbow on the mahogany desk top in front of him. His eyes did not flicker. "Mr. Coleman?"

"Judge, we vigorously oppose this motion. I've seen the plaintiff. I took his deposition. He was perfectly able to answer questions. Yes, he was in a wheelchair, but he was able to lie to me, in response to the very first question, and he kept it up, lying throughout the deposition."

"Spoken like a partisan. Mr. Coleman, you never disappoint. But leave the unnecessary accusations out of it."

"Sorry, Judge." Jimmy nodded and smiled, just to show he wasn't troubled by the judge's warning. All the black-suited Booker and Bayne associates smiled too.

"But what I'm trying to say," Jimmy went on, "is that there's no need for a preferential setting. And it's unfair to the other plaintiffs and defendants on your Honor's docket, if you give this plaintiff a boost to the front of the line, ahead of plaintiffs who've been waiting longer. And I can guarantee there are some of them, who are hurt more than this Mr. Grant."

Sammy Stubarsky was nodding his head like a dribbled basketball. "That's right, your Honor. And I might add, your Honor, that I represent two other plaintiffs with serious injuries. We'd be hard pressed to be ready for a preferential setting, even as plaintiffs, if it came up as early as Mr. Herrick seems to want."

Robert looked at Sammy sharply and then snapped his attention back to the judge.

"Your Honor, we have attached an affidavit from Mr. Grant's doctor to the motion for preferential setting. The doctor says, and I quote, that *we simply cannot be sure that his injury will not cause death to Mr. Grant at any particular time.*"

"You can say that about just about any of us." Jimmy's voice sounded like too-hard chalk on a roughened blackboard. "I'm not sure I'll be alive at any particular time, myself. I've stopped growing upwards from the top and started growing outwards from the middle. That's life-threatening too."

The judge smiled. And there was a moment of indecision.

"I'll tell you what," said Manny Lopez finally. "I'm going to enter an order that all of you must meet with a mediator. If the case is like what you say it's like, Mr. Herrick, I bet it will settle, when a mediator gets everyone to negotiate. And Mr. Coleman, you give Mr. Herrick your best possible offer beforehand, and then, you continue to be generous."

"The soul of giving. That's me." Delay is the defense lawyer's best friend, and so Jimmy spread his dirty smile.

"Mr. Herrick, I'm going to deny your motion. At least for now. If you just can't settle this case, file another motion for a preferential setting and I'll look at it."

"Yes, your Honor," Robert said flatly.

"But meanwhile, there's no reason why this case can't be settled." The judge glared at Jimmy, then at Robert, then back at Jimmy, and again at Robert. "So. Go settle it!"

* * *

When Robert told him they didn't have a preferential setting, William Grant seemed surprisingly upbeat.

"What exactly does it mean?" he asked.

Robert was gloomy. "It's going to be a longer time than we had hoped, before we can go to trial."

"But meanwhile, we get to argue the case in front of a mediator?"

"That's right."

"Well, maybe we can settle it. You've told me about the possibility of settling the case. Maybe the other side will pay what they ought to. And as you've explained, the mediator is there to help us settle it."

"That's right."

"So maybe the time will be shorter. Maybe this means we'll get it done quicker."

"Well, William, I'm glad you feel this way. I've been kind of down about it. But you're right, of course."

"And if we don't settle it with a mediator, we can ask for a preferential early trial setting again, right?"

"That's right."

"Sounds okay to me."

"But I've been concerned about your health, William. And so are you, of course."

"Yes. Very concerned. But I guess I'll just have to concentrate on staying alive. I'll have to fight to keep the infection bugs away." The man in the wheelchair smiled.

Robert smiled too. Some clients are difficult, he told himself. But some clients aren't.

And some clients actually make it easier to do the job.

17

The mediator was fat, short, and bald. He wore a gray jacket that did not quite match his gray pants, and his tie had ink spots among the dots that were supposed to be there. His spectacles were old-time lined bifocals, and he wore them on a chain around his neck. He was a retired judge who, during his active years, had been known to run a tough, no-nonsense courtroom. Now, however, he wheezed and hesitated.

His opening speech was standard, but way too long. This was a welcoming environment, he declared. A warm environment. You could say anything while trying to settle the case, and no one outside the room would ever know it. His job was just to act as "an advocate for settlement," with no power to impose anything. He was on everyone's side and no one's side. He repeated these thoughts a dozen times in slightly different words.

His questions about what he called "the three required commitments" were also standard: Would the plaintiff seriously try to settle the case? Would the defendant? Would both sides continue the effort unless and until the mediator declared an impasse? Would both sides listen to each other?

Both sides answered yes, we will. With responses that were mechanical and perfunctory, because the questions were also mechanical and perfunctory.

Finally, the man in the mismatched gray outfit ended his stemwinder of a speech. "Now, let's hear from the plaintiff," he said, with a warm smile.

Robert put his notes down. "By now, we've taken the depositions of five personnel at Blackminster Construction Company, including the crane operator, in addition to Gunther Blackminster. There's no question about the negligence of Blackminster in this accident."

He held up his index finger. "Number one, the crane operator was inexperienced. He'd never done the job before." Then, two fingers. "He was given no instruction, in spite of the difficulty of using this particular crane, which everyone else knew." Three fingers. "Third, he was grossly underpaid for the job, which Gunther Blackminster did not directly admit, but he did admit that an experienced gentleman would be paid more than twice as much." Four fingers. "Blackminster knew that the crane mechanism was defective, that it stuck and stopped and started unpredictably, but they neither repaired it nor got this inexperienced operator ready for it."

He took his fingers down. "And all of that spells negligence. There are other acts of negligence described in our amended suit papers, but those four will do for now."

Next, he described the accident and how it was affected by the negligence of Gunther Blackminster and of the crane owner, the Janowitz Company. And then, he was ready to talk about damages.

"As you know, a cut into the abdomen is a terribly, horribly painful injury. It was a medieval torture technique, to cut a victim in the abdomen. Mr. Grant has suffered unspeakable pain, which is part of his damages. He still has that pain, and he'll have it for the rest of his life. He had a good job, with good pay and benefits, but he cannot work any longer, in spite of having tried to find various kinds of jobs. In other words, he has lost earnings that are enormous, both past and future." Robert paused, to let that sink in. Then: "His medical expenses are also huge, and those are part of his damages too. Finally, he cannot do the things he used to do that provide satisfaction in life. He cannot go to a football game or play tennis. And what we call his 'loss of consortium' with his wife is part of his damages too."

He looked directly at Gunther Blackminster, and then at Jimmy Coleman. "If we go to trial, we will have more than thirty witnesses, including doctors, therapists, and a labor economist. And that's our case."

Robert usually thought that the client should say something, very brief but emotional, and he had readied the man sitting beside him.

And so he said, "Mr. Grant, what can you add to that?"

The voice of the man in the wheelchair was a mixture of anger and sorrow. "These guys were careless as all get out." He shook his head. "Negligent, is what the law calls it. Unforgivable, is what anybody else would call it. And I'm not a lawyer, so I don't know about the legal definition of damages, but let me just say this. They hurt me very badly."

Perfect, thought Robert.

The mediator spoke. "And so, Mr. Herrick, what is your opening demand, in dollars?"

His answer was firm. "We believe that the damages will exceed ten million dollars. We would like to settle it, and so that is our offer. Ten million dollars."

* * *

Sammy Stubarsky sat on the plaintiffs' side of the table, with his two clients. But his opening statement was strange, for a plaintiff. "We agree that the defendants were negligent. But William Grant was also negligent, more negligent than the defendants. And he exaggerates his damages. My clients were not negligent, and they are hurt as bad as William Grant."

And that was it, from Sammy.

Robert was astounded as he stared at the other plaintiffs' lawyer. Oh, well, he thought. Sometimes plaintiffs don't agree. But Sammy's remarks seemed way off base. For one thing, his clients showed no signs of any continuing injury like William Grant's.

What is going on? he asked himself.

* * *

Jimmy Coleman's speech was predictable. William Grant was negligent. William Grant was the heart and soul of negligence. And his injuries were not nearly as bad as he claimed. The plaintiff's lawyers had inflated them.

"The damages are pumped up beyond recognition!" Jimmy's voice sounded like an off-center table saw.

Jimmy turned his dead-fish eyes toward William Grant. "We sincerely regret the fact that you got hurt at all that day. But we vigorously, absolutely deny that it was our fault. Instead, it was your fault."

He smiled his dirty smile. "We want to settle any case we can. Including this one. Given the amount you were hurt, and we believe it was minimal, we will make an offer to settle. Our offer is one hundred thousand dollars."

The mediator smiled too. So, the plaintiff demanded ten million dollars, and the defendants offered to pay only a hundred thousand? In other words, one percent of what the plaintiffs asked?

But the mediator had seen cases settle, even though the two sides had started far apart. So had the lawyers.

Jimmy turned toward Sammy Stubarsky. "We'll offer the same amounts to each of your clients. A hundred thousand each. We recognize that each of the three plaintiffs had minor injuries."

* * *

The next step, for the mediator, was to separate the parties into different spaces called "caucus rooms." And for the remainder of the mediation, he would trudge back and forth among them. A kind of "shuttle diplomacy." He would rip apart each side's assumptions, show them the weaknesses in their positions, and urge them, push them, and cajole them into making new offers, for amounts that were increasingly closer to settling the case.

"I've just met with Jimmy Coleman and his clients," the mediator announced as he entered the caucus room where Robert waited with William Grant. "I'm pleased to tell you that Jimmy Coleman asked me to say that he really wants to settle this case and will go the extra mile."

"Well," Robert drawled, "that's nice. But now, the important thing is, what's his number?"

"He's showing good movement. If you settle now, Mr. Coleman is offering one million dollars." The mediator smiled. "I did a little terrorism to him."

Mediators! Robert thought. They always think they're the most important people at a mediation, getting everything done. Jimmy surely wasn't "terrorized."

"Well, okay," he answered slowly. "We'll counter by offering to take nine million five hundred thousand."

"Oh, give me a little more than that," said the mediator quickly. "Because Jimmy's right, you know. Any jury is going to say that Mr.

Grant was contributorily negligent. You could lose this case. And Mr. Grant, I hope you take it as a compliment when I say that you look to be in pretty good shape. Nine million is way above the damages you'd get."

A mediator will say a lot of things to settle a case.

"Well, maybe nine million, four hundred thousand. We'll give you a hundred thousand more, Mr. Mediator. Is that okay, William?"

"It's not enough, but I'll take it to the defendants," said the mediator in a sour voice.

* * *

The afternoon dragged by with visit after visit by the mediator. The opposing sides moved closer, by inches. At four o'clock, the defendants were offering two million dollars and the plaintiffs were offering to settle for eight-and-one-half million.

"You told me not to come back asking for any more reductions," said the mediator to Robert, at five o'clock. "Well, this time I'm not asking. I'm *begging!*"

Actually, Robert thought, I may have underestimated this mediator. He's doing the job. Or trying hard, at least.

"Can't you go down to eight million?" The mediator really was begging, now. "Or, can you do that if I tell the other side you'll go down to that if they make a big move?"

"What do you think, William?"

"Okay. But Mr. Mediator, only tell them the amount of eight million if they make a big move."

"Yes. I'll try my best."

* * *

At eleven o'clock at night, the two sides were still far apart. Robert and his client were asking for eight million. The defendants had offered two and a half million. And what was more important, neither side had moved for hours on end. The mediator had gotten everyone together in the central room again, separated them again, offered his own suggested settlement figure, and pulled and tugged constantly at each side.

There was no change.

"I'm going to declare an impasse," said the mediator finally. "But I'm going to ask each side to continue negotiating and to keep the offers open."

Sometimes, in the cold light of dawn, or after a few days of thinking, the parties will magically come together. And settle. Even after a mediation.

"Well, William, I'm sorry," Robert said as he packed his file to leave. "We're back to square one."

Jimmy Coleman walked by with his entourage. "Thanks for holding out and setting us up to try this one, Herrick. You got another worthless, piece-a-shit case, and we're gonna stick it into you and break it off."

18

The night of the mediation, Robert fell into a deep sleep. He was all right until he dreamed he saw William Grant back in the hospital again. Then he saw Jimmy Coleman. Then, for no apparent reason, he found himself staring at a huge wave of spiders that were as big as dogs. Hundreds of them. He woke up tangled in a spider's web so tight that he couldn't bend it. As he recovered his sight, he gradually saw that the web was made of bed sheets.

Maria was concerned. "What's the matter, Robert? *What's the matter?*"

He was awake now, and he grinned. "Dealing with Jimmy Coleman leads to bad dreams. That's all."

"Yes. I understand that."

An hour later, he was walking into his office with the dream forgotten, but with a lingering distaste for cases against Jimmy Coleman.

* * *

Across town, about the same time, two sometimes adversaries were planning to combine against Robert Herrick's lawsuit.

The table at the main bar of the River Oaks Country Club furnished a magnificent setting for Gunther Blackminster to meet the union president. The little, unkempt man who sat across from him had a green plaid jacket and a gray tie. He drank the house bourbon, which was actually pretty good here. Blackminster, who was a big man with sandy hair in a charcoal pinstriped suit, drank an excellent Scotch. Lagavulin, to be precise.

"Well," the union president said slowly, "what's gonna happen to this hyere law suit? How much damage they gonna load your heinie with, from losin?"

"Maybe eight million? Ten million? Possibly. And we don't have that kind of insurance. It could put us under."

"Seriously?"

"Yeah, seriously."

"You think you'd be in bad enough quicksand so you might lose it?"

"I don't have any idea. I can figure construction jobs. I can figure payrolls. But not lawsuits. I'm not so good at figuring those out."

"What's your lawyer say?"

"Well, everybody knows Jimmy Coleman. He's over-the-top confident about how we're gonna stomp all over the other side. But when push comes to shove, he's willing to settle it for two and a half million. And he says we have what he calls . . . *some expo-o-o-sure.*" Blackminster dragged the word out, expo-o-o-sure, the way he'd heard Jimmy say it. "That's legalese for saying, we could easily lose this case and owe a huge amount."

"Well, Mister Blackminster, we can't be havin a op'ration like yours go bust."

"Right. From my point of view, it's the company I founded and built, which would be a complete loss. It would be like the death of one of your children. No, not quite the same, but you understand. And from your point of view at the union, it's also very bad. That's a lot of jobs lost."

"Yeah. Damn right. So. What 'cha gonna do about it?"

"Well, that's what I wanted to talk to you about. To the union. We're gonna fight the case, of course. We've got Jimmy Coleman representing us, 'cause he's the meanest son of a bitch in the valley. He's costing a ton of money, and he always has a whole circus full of these dark-suited juniors following him around, and they also cost a ton. But we gotta do it. But beyond that . . . , well, that's what I wanted to talk to you about. About getting some help from the union."

"We got the same goals here, is what you're sayin."

"That's right. The public thinks we at management and you folks in labor are at each other's throats. Sometimes, I guess. But mosta the time, we got the same goals. And for sure, we do here."

"Well, on behalf of the union, I seen your point. I can guarantee we'd like to help."

"I knew you would."

"Maybe we can discourage this lawsuit. Maybe we, the union, can reason with the plaintiff's lawyers. They say this guy Robert Herrick is smart. In fact, I think our own steward at your business sent Little Willie Grant to Robert Herrick. He referred him, the union steward."

"Yeah. That's my understanding."

"Maybe we can reason with Mr. Herrick. And discourage this lawsuit. Or at least, maybe we can get him to be a little more reasonable."

"I tell you one thing for damn sure," said Blackminster firmly. "I don't wanna know *anything* about what you're doing, when you're . . . *persuading* Mr. Herrick, or what your methods are, to try to get that done."

"No." The union president grinned. "That's fo' sure. You don't wanna know."

* * *

Wendy Bachman sat at her customary perch in front of the appellate lawyers' offices inside the District Attorney's building. "So, good job, Maria. The Court of Appeals affirmed the death sentence for this guy. The one who did all the robbery murders with clerks and random customers lying on the floor, and he shot them in the back of the head. This rat-fucker named *Landers.*"

"I figured the Court of Appeals would go with us in this case. But hey, you never know."

"And you predicted that the Supreme Court would be fast in refusing to hear the case. And here, pretty damn quick, they've entered the usual one sentence order saying, it's denied."

"Nothing novel enough in this case for the Supreme Court. The arguments the defense lawyers are down to, now, are like a Hail Mary pass."

"Nobody celebrates an execution," said the secretary known as "the cussing Mormon," who always had her big-print Bible on her desk. "But nobody deserves it more than this crazy bastard."

"Well, I'd use kinder words, I guess, but . . . that's right, Wendy. Totally ridiculous, unnecessary, cruel murders, and a lot of them."

"What's next?"

"We'll ask the trial judge to set an execution date. And to set it early. The earlier it is, the fewer kinds of new Hail Marys we'll see."

"It's got to be a certain minimum amount of time, doesn't it?"

"Yes. That's so that the defense lawyers can go to the Parole Board, to the Governor, and even back to the courts if they have something that's not been ruled on. It's for fairness. But the problem is, they'll go to all those places, and they'll do their best to raise complicated issues where they can be selective with the facts, or even whitewash the facts, so the courts or the parole board or the Governor or whoever else has to take a lot of time to sort through it and order delays."

"And . . . what do you think, O Maximum Boss Maria?"

"I think this defendant is bad enough, and the case is solid enough, and the arguments are already picked over enough, so that even if we don't celebrate executions, we'll see justice done. As it should be, in this instance. It is richly deserved."

19

The big conference room at the offices of Robert Herrick and Associates was almost as wide as a basketball court. The walls were hung with museum-quality paintings, and a long oriental rug stretched under the big mahogany table. The conference room was a product of strategy, a tool of the trade, designed to impress visitors, especially opponents, of the prowess of this plaintiff's law firm.

Today, the room was filled nearly to capacity. There were lawyers, witnesses, clients, and assorted hangers-on, because today was the day to begin depositions of the expert witnesses in the case of *Grant v. Blackminster Construction Company*. The early witnesses would mostly be doctors. Later, there would be experts on crane maintance and crane operation.

Jimmy Coleman was resplendent in a tan suit. His Rolex President was a half pound of gold and diamonds, and he wore cuff links that you could see sparkling from two blocks away. This was to be a deposition of Jimmy's hired doctor, who would be questioned by the plaintiff's lawyers.

"And what opinions did you formulate after you reviewed the documents, Doctor?" Robert Herrick asked. He was dressed more modestly, in a brown jacket and gray slacks.

The witness smiled indulgently, to signal that it seemed like a silly question to him. "Anyone would arrive at a diagnosis of peritoneal penetrating trauma," he said quickly, "with injuries to various structures, as one would expect. A significant loss of blood led to shock and unconsciousness. Because the patient was treated promptly, the bleeding itself caused no lasting outcome. There was a subsequent diagnosis of infection with Bacteriodes Fragilis and other pathogens. That minor illness was treated successfully in a short time."

So far the doctor had used a lot of words to say nothing that everyone didn't already know. But everyone around the table also recognized what this witness's job was. Jimmy had employed him to minimize the seriousness of William Grant's injuries. He would treat them as no big deal, a blip on the curve along a normal life. And, of course, the doctor had been coached to say as little as possible that could inform the plaintiff's lawyers of anything.

Robert knew this, and so he persisted. "All right, Doctor. Did you form any other opinions?"

"Yes. That the patient had a good prognosis."

This statement, which meant only that William Grant allegedly had a "good future," was vague enough to be useless.

"And what other opinions did you reach, Doctor?"

"Although the patient uses a wheelchair, he does not need to use it on a continuous basis. He can walk. With physical therapy, he will regain his ability to walk in a normal manner."

No question about it; this doctor was Jimmy Coleman's hired expert.

"And what other opinions?"

"That's about it." The doctor flashed a beaming smile. A bedside-manner smile.

And so, Robert thought, I'm going to have to dig for his opinions. Like a dentist pulling teeth.

"Doctor, what structures sustained injuries in Mr. Grant's body, and what were the injuries to each body part?"

The question was worded to minimize the advantage of a vague or incomplete answer. If the doctor left anything out, the omission would be used to impeach his testimony at trial.

"There were injuries to the skin, of course, first of all. And to the abdominal muscles, the peritoneal sac, various nerves, the pancreas, the spleen, the liver. Each of those suffered lacerations. The small intestine suffered multiple lacerations and ruptures, and so did the large intestine."

The next set of questions established that the Doctor, along with every other member of the medical community, considered the liver to be "a delicate organ," and that lacerations there "could be considered by some to be a significant problem." Then, Robert led the doctor through all of the other injured structures. Each answer contained specifics that would be used before the jury to contradict the doctor. To show, contrary to this doctor's bought-and-paid-for opinion, that the injuries were serious and permanent.

And then the doctor had to justify each of his opinions with sources and reasons. The prediction of William Grant's "good future," in particular, turned out to have little support other than wishful thinking. In fact, the doctor finally conceded, the injury had shortened the plaintiff's life expectancy by "a substantial number of years."

"That's all. I pass the witness," said Robert at last. It was a good deposition, he thought.

But then, he had a second thought. It was a good deposition . . . *maybe*. On the other hand . . . *maybe not*. He felt that something was wrong. Was there a big issue that he had not discovered, one that could ruin his case, something he hadn't known to ask about? And more immediately, what would happen when Jimmy Coleman questioned the plaintiff's own doctors?

Jimmy would be just as thorough as Robert, and more brutal.

* * *

Lester Landers's last meal was three cheeseburgers with fries. And a Coke.

In earlier times, the Department of Criminal Justice had given condemned prisoners whatever they wanted, if it could be found. The present rule was, anything available in the prison kitchen. Cheeseburger-and-Coke last meals were frequent favorites, then and now.

At five o'clock, a guard appeared to ask Mr. Landers, "Do you want a sedative?" It is a question asked everyone awaiting execution. And every single convict facing execution accepts. Always. One theory is that condemned prisoners needed something to help them face their fear. A more widely held belief was that they liked taking drugs.

Promptly at six o'clock, they came for Lester Landers again. For the man who had committed so many murders during robberies. Inside the death house, he was no longer handcuffed, no longer in a belly chain. "It's time," they said.

He rose and shook himself. Slowly, but deliberately. It is uncommon for condemned prisoners to resist the short walk to the end of the hall. The ethic among these killers is to "take it like a man."

The walls of the small, very old room are brick, but they are painted a bright, cheerful blue. The gurney is stark white. It has two flat arms that reach out from the central bedding on which the prisoner will recline, and it looks disconcertingly like a cross.

Lester Landers knew his role, and he took his place on the gurney. The tie-down team had his legs and arms encircled by straps in less than a minute. The men on this team had practiced the maneuver, and they were able to complete it quickly. A prison worker—not a doctor, because the Hippocratic oath forbids it—found a vein in the prisoner's arm and established an intravenous flow.

To Landers's right, there were big windows. The warden held up a hand, and the curtains opened. In the far space, the condemned man could see his witnesses: the ones he had invited. There were his sister, his nephew, his lawyers—and Margene Landers, his wife. He had married her while on death row, after they had met through letters and occasional conversations.

In the nearer window, there were survivors of the men and women he had killed. They could see him, and he could see them. These family members wore curious looks: mixtures of disgust and weariness. Behind them, because she did not want to interfere with the families, stood Maria Melendes, the DA's Official Killer, doing the last part of her job.

"Do you have anything to say?" asked the warden.

The condemned man stirred. And finally spoke. "To those who I hurt, I am sorry. I pray to the Lord that what happens today will bring some peace to you. I am in His loving arms right now."

The man on the gurney paused. Then: "To my dear family, I love you. Don't nobody be sad. What's done is done. I made choices. We all make choices, and there are consequences, and that's all that's happening today. To Margene, you are the love of my life and always will be. I thank God for you."

He turned, then, toward the warden. "Lock and load. Let's do it, man."

The warden, at this point, usually pauses momentarily. And then gives a signal. At this time, it was taking off his glasses.

No one could see what was happening next. The drug was not immediately lethal. Phenobarbital, which is a tangled combination of carbon, nitrogen, hydrogen, and oxygen, acts first as an anesthetic. It was administered in a dose that would also cause coma. And then it would stop Lester Landers's heart. He gurgled, now, and expelled several heavy breaths. Then he was still.

A little over ten minutes later, a doctor pronounced Lester Landers dead.

A little over twenty minutes after that, Maria Melendes trudged out of the witness room, behind the victims' survivors. By now, she felt a weight off her shoulders, but at the same time, she felt immensely, ferociously, viciously tired.

And overwhelmingly sad. All she could think of was the disjointed conversation, the tears, and the faces of the family members she had stood with.

* * *

The next morning, it was Jimmy Coleman's turn to take the deposition of William Grant's doctor.

"Doctor," Jimmy croaked, "you were here during the time that Robert Herrick took the deposition of that other doctor yesterday, right?"

"Well . . . yes, sir."

"You agree with what he said, don't you?"

A pause. "Well . . . yes, sir."

Robert had prepared the doctor for this deposition, but he hadn't expected this question. Most lawyers wouldn't.

Jimmy was delighted. "Well, in that case, I can just as well finish this deposition right now!"

He shuffled his papers, as if to pack them away. But then:

"Doctor, just a few more questions."

And with that, far from declaring the deposition finished, Jimmy kept the doctor answering questions for another five hours. What were his conclusions or opinions? Is that all of them? What about opinions about this? Or this? And what were the factors behind each opinion? What were the factors behind the factors? And several times, even, what were the factors behind those factors?

How could the doctor possibly answer the following argument, without sounding like a quack? How could he rely on such-and-such factor and keep his license to practice medicine?

It was ugly to watch, because the doctor was not the type to argue back. He was accustomed to more polite conversation. And Jimmy was very effective. The answers he pulled from this deposition would help him to persuade the jury that William Grant's injury was much less serious than he claimed.

* * *

Sammy Stubarsky was entitled to ask questions too. And he did. Just one question.

"Doctor, what you're saying is that William Grant isn't hurt as badly as his lawyers are claiming. Is that right?"

"Well, an injury to the abdomen usually looks spectacular, but sometimes it isn't nearly as bad as it looks. Still, Mr. Grant is hurt pretty badly."

It was a strange question, because Sammy's clients were the other two plaintiffs, and it didn't seem to help them at all.

Robert Herrick shook his head as he walked out of the conference room with Tom Kennedy. "A very wise man told me, '*Some guys pull tricks instead of doing it the usual way. Watch them and you know how to beat them.*'"

He paused. "But I'll be darned if I can figure out how that applies to Sammy Stubarsky."

"Nothing's ever easy," was all Tom said.

20

Across town at Booker and Bayne's offices, dozens of lawyers were talking about the crane-hook case. Their theories about the best way to defend at trial echoed all over the white birch corridors. There were only a few days to go.

When Jimmy Coleman arrived, he went immediately to the big conference room and sat with his trial team. Nearly a dozen black-suited lawyers surrounded the polished marble table. Portraits of partners covered the white walls, with Colonel Henry Anderson Booker over the head position, where Jimmy sat. The Colonel looked out silently and sternly, with a stark, pinched face featuring rimless glasses framing searching eyes, above a midnight blue suit and a dark blue tie that just missed being black.

"My friends, we are honored today to have Dr. Murphy with us." Jimmy gestured toward the psychologist who sat nearby. "Many of you know him, because if we're about to try a big one, we usually get Dr. Murphy to advise us. As you know, this is the age of consultants, and Dr. Murphy is the best there is."

The man who stood, at that, had coke-bottle glasses and a head as bald as a frankfurter. He looked like a jolly genie standing beside the TV monitor with a collapsible metal pointer in his hand. He wore a purple-and-gray plaid jacket that was pasted across his chubby frame too tightly, together with tan flannel slacks and his trademark Hush-Puppy-style footwear.

One of the black suits whispered, almost loud enough for the Great Man himself to hear, "Dr. Murphy could benefit from consulting a clothing psychiatrist himself, to tone down that crazy wardrobe."

"There's no question about this man's value to us," Jimmy went on. "So please pay attention. He can tell you whether Republican lesbians would be quick to acquit a big-time inside trader, or whether Lutherans would be lenient on a negligent trucking company."

Dr. Murphy laughed and looked like a man trying to look modest.

"Thank you, Mr. Coleman. And all of you are lucky to be working with such a skillful trial lawyer. Mr. Coleman is the master."

Now it was Jimmy who was trying unsuccessfully to look humble.

"As most of you know, Litigation Consultants—that's my firm—we work a lot with what are called 'focus groups.' These are groups of people we hire to predict what juries would do. A focus group has to be diverse, with people of different races and religions, and different jobs or positions. Usually, we use five or six people. More than that, you suppress some of their willingness to speak, and you get distortion. Fewer, you no longer have the diversity you need."

He pushed a button, and the screen flicked to life, with the words "Litigation Consultants" in big letters beside a catchy logo. Another twitch against the button, and the particulars appeared to describe the focus group that was coming up.

"As you see, this covers the focus group that was used on this particular date. It was composed of a retired electrician, a schoolteacher, an unemployed woman, a college student, and a musician. We try to get people currently in jobs because they tend to be jury leaders, but it's almost impossible with managers and professionals, and it's sometimes retired people instead. There was one black woman and a Latino man."

Dr. Murphy changed the screen again. "As this slide says, we showed the group a film that summarized the evidence, composed of deposition excerpts, exhibits, and narration that stitched it together. The film was made neutrally, or as neutrally as we could do it, so that it didn't tilt what the expected evidence is going to be. And of course, we didn't tell anyone which side had hired us."

Another push of the button changed the screen again. "We gave the jury two arguments, one by the plaintiff and one by the defendant. The focus group members had electronic dials that we could trace on an ongoing basis, showing how much they agreed with the arguments. Now, let me play the arguments. And below them, you will see the traces showing percentage of agreement."

The argument for the defendant began. The first position was, "The crane did not have serious deficiencies." The trace remained low, meaning low credibility in that argument.

Dr. Murphy froze the film. "What this means is that you won't be successful if you take the position that the crane was in good shape."

He switched back to the screen. "In any event," went the following argument, "every crane is differently adjusted, and cranes are always difficult to operate." The trace went much higher.

Again, Dr. Murphy touched a button, and the film stopped. "The better approach is to say that cranes are just finicky, hard-to-operate equipment."

". . . The plaintiff in this case who had his back turned, William Grant, failed to take good care of his own safety." And with this argument, the trace went to its highest point.

"Your best approach," said Dr. Murphy, "is to attack the plaintiff."

An hour and a half later, the film ended with interviews of the five focus group members, and Jimmy said, "Okay. This has been exactly what the doctor ordered. We have the background for our strategy."

He turned to the psychologist. "Thank you, Dr. Murphy." And then, to his black-suited associates: "Now, let's figure out how to present our evidence so that we can make the best use of what the good doctor has taught us."

* * *

But Booker and Bayne was not the only group using jury consultants. So did the plaintiffs' lawyers. Beneath the greenhouse-style windows in his office, Robert Herrick sat with Tom Kennedy over the multi-colored oriental carpet. They held copies of a report from a consulting firm called Calkins Jurimetrics.

Professor Alistair Calkins was the head of the Department of Sociology at Rice University, but he made most of his income preparing reports like this one. The cover of the document said, "Jury Selection Recommendations for the Trial of the Crane-Hook Case: A Survey and Analysis."

"You know, Robert." Tom looked out the window to the green surrounding Buffalo Bayou, past the point where it merged with the green of Memorial Park, and toward the vague line where it blended into the gray of the horizon. "I'm always skeptical of these kinds of reports. We can't take this advice from Professor Calkins too seriously."

"And we won't," Robert agreed. "Everyone knows, including Professor Calkins, that an experienced lawyer can cut a jury better than the smartest psychologist. A guy who has tied his shoes a thousand times is better at tying them than someone who never has, and who has only studied in a book about how to tie his shoes."

"Some of this stuff sounds crazy."

"Well, Professor Calkins is an old hand at this. And I've always found that he tends to be reliable."

"Here it is, for instance. The report says, 'Young people and older people tend to be more sympathetic to the plaintiff. Middle-aged people are more likely to side with the defendant.'"

"Well, yes. It's a telephone survey, based on a scenario given to the people who Dr. Calkins and his people called. He's not saying that every middle-aged guy is against us, or that every young person is for us. That's why he uses words like 'tend' and 'more likely.'"

"Our plaintiff is middle-aged, I guess. Depending on what you think 'middle-aged' means. Some of them might look at William Grant and see themselves."

"That's right. And that's why we will take Dr. Calkins's advice together with our own instincts. There might very well be a middle-aged man or woman that we'd want to keep on the jury because they identify with our client."

"Well . . . I guess."

"What it shapes up as, we want jurors who have people-pleasing occupations. A beautician. A shoe salesman. Dr. Calkins is saying that managers and professional people tend to be against us. Catholics and Jewish people are good for us, and mainline protestant people are less so."

"Then, our ideal juror is a beautician who is Catholic or Jewish."

"Well, yes. But it always depends, on exactly the kinds of factors you've pointed out, Tom."

"I . . . don't know."

"And actually, Dr. Calkins says that if we can get professional or managerial people who we think are in our favor, they are very desirable jurors."

"I missed that. Why?"

Robert smile. "Big damages. Professional and managerial people tend to award bigger damages, if they do find that the defendant is liable."

"Okay. I guess that makes sense. Professional and managerial folks make more money, so they think in terms of more money."

"Right."

"As far as that goes," Tom grinned too, "I suppose we would want Warren Buffett, who is one of the richest investors in America, and who seems to identify with the little guy more than the average zillionaire. That is, *if* Warren Buffet happens to be Catholic or Jewish. We'd have to find out."

"It doesn't really sound crazy. It sounds like one of the mysteries of psychology."

"And, well, big damages," Tom agreed, "that's something we want our jury to be thinking about."

21

Sammy Stubarsky's desk drowned in piles of paper. They overflowed on the floor. Most were typed white pages, but there was one disheveled stack that was yellowish and one that was green. A winding pathway stretched from the desk chair to the door, and along its edges the piles had begun to mix, so that it was impossible to say where one ended and another began.

Now, Sammy stared absentmindedly out the window, because he was waiting for an incoming call. He was only mildly interested in what was on the computer monitor. But he glanced there occasionally to see a group of pornographic images in a range of coupled positions. He had spread some white powder on the desk in one of the few open spaces, and he turned to arranging it in lines with a pen that carried the name, "Shady Delight Massage Parlor." The words below that name were, "We'll make you smile."

Using a straw, Sammy inhaled the first line of cocaine. The sound of his telephone startled him, because it rang at the same time that his senses started to expand. He fumbled to pick it up. "Hello?"

"Mr. Stubarsky!" The voice creaked, but it sounded friendly. "Jimmy Coleman here."

A pause. "Oh. Hello, sir. I've been expectin to hear from you. How are you?"

"Fine, fine, and I hope the same for you, my friend."

"We're gonna work out this case we got, Mr. Coleman."

"Absolutely. But no deals."

"No deals."

"I think we understand each other."

"Yes, sir."

"Now, I wanted to let you know, yesterday was the last day to designate your expert doctor." Jimmy's voice sputtered like an outboard motor.

"Yes, sir."

"And as far as I know, you haven't designated any doctor, and that could ruin your case. No deals, but I'm trying to be helpful." Jimmy cleared his throat. He sounded like an avalanche of gravel, to Sammy's overextended senses.

"Ahhh . . . maybe I haven't gotten around to that detail, or that— um, whaddyacallit—that nuance."

"Well, we're going to trial soon in this case. And you see, Sammy, if you don't have an expert doctor designated, it will be difficult to find a way for you to prove up your damages. I'd want to see you get paid, as we understand, but I can only do so much. You'd better designate a doc as fast as you can. Like, today. You ought to do it today."

"Yes, sir."

"If you do it today, I can overlook it and no one will be the wiser."

"Okay. I'll just file a paper saying that I designate the physicians who treated my two guys. I don't have the information in front of me. Do you happen to know it, Mr. Coleman?"

"I've got the file in front of me." It was usually foolish to designate only a treating physician, but it didn't matter in this case. Jimmy let it slide.

"Let me get a pencil." And Sammy wrote two doctors' names, addresses, telephones, and emails as Jimmy dictated them. "You'll need to add something to the effect that these doctors are going to testify about your clients' injuries and their future prospects."

"Yes, sir. I'm gonna get it done rapidly. Rapidly."

As soon as he rang off, Sammy called for his legal assistant. He gave her directions to insert his handwritten words into a document with the proper headings and designation and other verbiage, sign his name, and file it.

"Today, please. Remember. Today."

* * *

Robert saw Maria's nose wrinkle as soon as they entered Professor Perry Jones's luxury condominium on the fifteenth floor of Bayou

Bend Towers. The odor of cigarette smoke was overpowering. But the view out the window was even more spectacular than the one from Robert's office, all green and brown, with the slow meanders of Buffalo Bayou way down below. Robert knew how much Professor Jones loved this place, with raw, muddy nature outside, packaged beside beautiful amenities inside.

Robert also knew that whenever he had trouble with one of his cases, the irreverent Perry Jones could serve as an encyclopedia full of answers. The professor knew the tort cases in this state better than the Supreme Court justices did. And he always came at the solutions from a different perspective. Now, in this case, with his fellow plaintiff's lawyer acting strangely, Robert really needed Professor Jones, to help him figure out what was going on.

"Perry! Perry Jones!" He looked into the living room. "Are you here?"

Perry Jones had been Robert's favorite professor in law school. Unconventional. Iconoclastic. A lot of people didn't like him. But Perry Jones had forgotten more law than most professors ever knew.

"Robert Herrick! I'm here watching the ball game. How's it hangin', young fella?" Then, the professor saw Maria. "Oops! I shouldn't use such sorry-ass language." And he dissolved into a coughing fit of laughter.

Maria stared at him. She had met this professor once before, with Robert, but he was a sight. Almost bald, with a ring of white hair. He was sitting on a scooter that substituted for a wheelchair. His arms were skinny, but actually, they were way past skinny—they were spindly.

"Maria, you've met Professor Francis Perribone Jones before. Known to his friends as Perry Jones."

"Friends that don't include you, bucko." The professor gave out the same hacking laugh."Sit down, next to me, Miss Maria."

He looked her up and down. "Maria, how long since you've had some really good sex?"

"I told you he was unconventional," Robert said unnecessarily.

"None of your damn business!" She looked shocked. But she wasn't, because she laughed.

"Oh. Well, see, that's typical of what I get. Women reject me. 'Cause I'm a cripple. I was hoping you'd be an exception."

"He always says that, and he calls himself a cripple," Robert explained. "I told you, about how he had polio when he was in his twenties. But he's made a good life, and he chases girls with a lot of success, actually."

"Not enough success."

"But we're here because Perry can help with what's happening in the William Grant case. He's the guy who knows everything, like Mr. Spock on Star Trek. He is the one who designed our tort system, the way it is now. The negligence laws. Remember, they call Perry *The Father of Tort Reform*."

"I don't know how that could have happened," said the self-styled cripple. "Me being the 'Father of Tort Reform,' that is. Couldn't have been, because we used a rubber."

Maria laughed. Not Robert; he had heard it too many times.

"He always says that," Robert said, disapprovingly.

"I always say that," agreed the professor.

Robert acted disgusted. But it was a mock version of disgust. He had expected Perry Jones to have fun, the way he usually did.

"Stop being silly for just a second, Perry, and let me ask you something. I have a strange case, where there is another plaintiff's lawyer. And that plaintiff's lawyer acts like he's in cahoots with the defendant."

He sketched out the case for the professor.

"Well," said Perry Jones, "there are a million different kinds of agreements that opposing parties sometimes make, even though they're on opposite sides. And they hope to gang up on another party, who's the target."

"I know, but it's usually defendants who get together against another defendant, in a case where there are a lot of defendants being sued."

"Well, maybe so, usually. But there's no reason a plaintiff can't do it too. One plaintiff who isn't hurt so bad, helps the defendant, and the defendant is going to ensure that this plaintiff gets a big recovery. So the plaintiff helps the defendant beat the other plaintiff, who is the real one that's hurt."

"But in this case, they insist there's no agreement between them. And they don't seem like they're lying. Besides, if there is an agreement, and they lie about it, they're both foolish, because they could get disbarred for that."

"Right. Only thing I can think of is, they don't have an express deal, but they act so that they follow the same actions as a deal would call for."

"Come again?"

"They just coordinate their actions, without making an agreement to coordinate. It only works, of course, if they know each other well, the defendant and plaintiff who do the coordinating. And they have to have confidence, each of them, that the other will follow through."

"Can I expose their agreement?"

"Maybe not. Literally speaking, they don't have an agreement. At least not an express agreement. Sure, they've 'agreed,' in some silent way, to a combined strategy. You may just have to win the case against two adversaries."

Robert thought about that for a moment. Then: "It's true. Nothing's ever easy."

* * *

In the living room of the Herrick home on Willowick Drive, the late sun curled through wide plantation shutters. Tan carpeting covered the broad oak floor under two couches upholstered in heavy leather, and everything was surrounded by a dotted wallpaper. Robert and Maria sat watching the news.

Right after a commercial ended, Anchor John Moreno appeared with a bright, toothpaste-ad smile. "This next story makes us feel good. The City Advancement Corporation, that nonprofit organization that has done so much for our area, announced today that it was undertaking an improvement program for the three main buildings in our theatre district, a bigger program than ever before."

The anchor smiled again. "This fine organization's president, Gunther Blackminster, has let everyone know that the Advancement Corporation will create twenty percent more capacity in those theatre venues. The city will become an even more desirable destination for the arts."

"Gunther Blackminster?" Robert was surprised. "He's the president of the Advancement Corporation?"

"President Blackminster was elected this month to his office," John Moreno went on, "after years of service on this and other civic organizations."

Maria's nose wrinkled. "He's a sleazebag, isn't he?"

"Well, I don't know that. He's just an opponent in one of our lawsuits. Not every opponent is a sleazebag. I sure do wish he'd pay my client what he ought to, but I can't say that he doesn't deserve the honor of being president of the Advancement Corporation."

Suddenly, the land-line telephone rang. A too-loud sound. "Hello?" Robert answered.

As he did, he noticed that the caller ID showed his own office number.

"Robert Herrick?" The voice was unfamiliar. It also was low and angry.

"Yes, that's me."

"You're the guy who has that lawsuit against the Blackminster Company. It's a good company. What you're doing will ruin the company. And it'll lose jobs. It'll mean hundreds of layoffs."

"Excuse me? Who is this?"

"Let's just say I'm a friend of the company. From outside. Listen. You'd better listen. You will regret it if you don't get some sense into you. If you don't settle that case and get out of the way, I will see to it that you regret your actions."

Robert stared at the telephone receiver.

"Message delivered," said the voice. "Pay attention, or you won't like what happens." And the line went dead.

The caller ID still showed Robert's own office number.

"They routed the call through your own phone system," said Maria slowly. "It will be untraceable."

"Untraceable." Robert shook his head with bewilderment. "All I've done is file a lawsuit. It's just a lawsuit. They're insured. It's a proper cost of doing business, paying for the harm you cause by your negligence. Everybody knows that."

He realized that he sounded as if he were trying to convince himself of it.

"Call the police," Maria said.

* * *

The telephone rang almost as soon as he had left his message about this strange call. "Robert? This is Donnie. Detective Donnie Cashdollar. Me and Detective Slaughter are on our way."

He could hear the smile in the detective's voice as he said, "I see that you are up to your old ways again, Robert. Causin trouble!"

22

It was like old home week when the detectives arrived. Donnie Cashdollar shook Robert's hand and grinned. "How many cases we been in together, my friend?"

"Too many to count. You guys are my favorite cops, for sure."

He was pleased to see that these two partners still followed their strange dress code. Detective Cashdollar was a thorough mismatch, wearing brown corduroy trousers, a black jacket, a blue and white striped shirt, and a red tie with green dots. His usual eclectic attire. Detective Derrigan Slaughter, who happened to be a big, muscular black man, always dressed elegantly. And he was elegant today: a solid maroon tie, a smooth off-white shirt, and a charcoal suit, which fit him perfectly.

These two officers' contrasting appearances had been a standing joke at the station at one time. By now, the sight was familiar, and nobody mentioned it any more. But Robert always appreciated it.

"Okay," said Derrigan Slaughter slowly. "So, there ain't no specific threat by this here miss-*sterious* voice. At least, not to do no specific kinda thing. But this unknown gentleman is doin a lotta braggin on his threats about how you gonna regret it, you gonna *really* regret it, and I'm gonna *see* that you gonna regret it."

"That's right. And the guy made sure that I understood what he meant."

"Well, you done the right thing by callin us."

"Thanks."

"Okay." Detective Cashdollar shook his head. "I'm just trying to figure out what we can do. I mean, in addition to coming here now and expressing our sympathy. Which doesn't do a lot of good."

"But it ain't gonna be no instance of us providin so-called *protection*." Detective Slaughter's voice was flat. "We cain't do it, less'n the mayor hisself orders it. To sit a couple officers outside a home, it takes four shifts of two guys, and that takes eight guys outta service."

"I know," Robert said quietly.

"Police givin protection? That only happens in the movies," Slaughter added.

"But here's what we can do," Cashdollar added. "We're gonna make sure there is a patrol officer near here, especially in the evening from, say, six p.m. to six a.m. And we'll arrange a way to connect you directly to that officer."

"By the way," Slaughter said, "I assume you be packin some kinda protection here in yo' home. The kind that don't need to wait for no PO-leece officer to come."

Robert nodded. "I had to use it once before. It's a hazard I've anticipated, and a lot of lawyers anticipate, actually. I've got an assault rifle." Quickly, he added, "A *legal* one, and it's not modified to full automatic. And I've got a license."

Donnie-the-Mismatched-Detective grinned at that. "Yep. This is the wild west."

* * *

The next day was the pretrial conference for the case of *Grant v. Blackminster Construction Company*. It was part of motion day in Judge Manny Lopez's court, and it was one of more than thirty hearings to be completed that morning.

That meant that the pretrial conference was short.

"It's next week we're going to try this case," said the judge. "Are you ready, Mr. Herrick?"

"Almost, Judge. We've got several interrogatories that Mr. Coleman hasn't answered, hanging out there."

"Mr. Coleman, can you get those answered today?"

"By tomorrow, Judge, except there's one that's just plain irrelevant and would cost thousands of dollars to answer."

"Answer the three that you can by tomorrow."

"Yes, your Honor."

"Other than that, Mr. Coleman, you're ready?"

"Ready and rarin to go." Jimmy's voice sounded like a sprocket moving against a chain.

"Excellent. This case is now preferentially set, and I won't grant any motions for postponement."

The judge looked at the docket sheet for the next case, and the lawyers turned to go. But then:

"Wait a minute," said the judge quickly. "We're preferentially set for trial, but there's no reason you can't settle this case. I know, I know, you went to mediation and didn't settle. I'm ordering you to try again, right here in the courthouse, in the jury room, now."

The lawyers looked shell-shocked. Judges always want any case to settle, especially if it's complex. But this was unusual.

"Mr. Coleman, you made an offer to settle at the mediation, and I assume it was a generous offer."

"Ahhh . . . that's right, Judge."

"Double it."

Jimmy's jaw bounced.

"Mr. Herrick, I assume you made a demand at this mediation, and you pushed it down to a modest level."

Robert smiled. He saw where this was going. "Yes, your Honor."

"Cut it in half."

The judge grinned, to show that he wanted negotiations, but he didn't really intend to order how the lawyers should make offers. And he pointed. "Now, get in that jury deliberation room, both of you, and work on it. Let's settle this case." He was serious about that part of it.

* * *

Even Jimmy Coleman was laughing when he and his black-suited entourage joined Robert and Tom in the jury deliberation room. "I've seen judges try a lot of things to get lawyers to settle, but nothing quite like this."

Robert laughed too. "Well, Jimmy, how about doubling your offer?"

"First place, the judge didn't mean it literally!" Jimmy laughed again. "But nice try, by both him and you. Also, I can't do anything without the agreement of my client, of course."

"Neither of us can. But we can agree to recommend whatever we negotiate. So, you can't agree to recommend doubling it. How much can you increase it? And I'll answer your bid."

Jimmy hemmed and hawed for several long minutes before saying, "All right. All right. I'll agree to go up from two and a half million. And recommend three million."

Robert conferred with Tom, whispering in a corner. Then: "I'll agree to recommend seven and a half million. You came up a half million, and I'm coming down that same amount."

"Great. We're only four and a half million apart."

"Let's see what happens if we go another round. I always tell my associates, if you get fair settlement value, the ethical thing is to settle. The right thing. For the client."

An hour later, they had exchanged several movements toward the center. They also had exchanged a number of threats and humorous moments, and from Jimmy, there had been some bombast.

They left with the offers and counteroffers still sitting at four million apart. "Look, there's only three million in insurance," Jimmy finally said. "You know that. The kind of numbers you're still talking would put Blackminster Construction into bankruptcy."

"We'll see," was all Robert could say. "I hear that all the time, of course, and it takes getting a judgment to find out."

But he had an uneasy feeling that Jimmy wasn't bluffing, at least this time.

23

oday was the day. The trial date. A uniformed "jury shepherd"—a deputy sheriff assigned to guide the jury panel—led a line of citizens to the front of the courtroom and sat eight of them in the first row. Then another eight in the second. Gradually, he filled the center section of the courtroom with potential jurors.

Spectators were buzzing. News reporters were taking notes. Judge Manny Lopez was looking on with a candidate-for-election smile, because these were not just members of a jury panel. They also were voters, and he was running for re-election.

"Good morning, ladies and gentlemen." His smile grew wider. "The case on trial today is called *Grant v. Blackminster Construction Corporation.* This is a civil case, which will be tried before a jury."

Tom whispered to Robert, "Judge Lopez is reading the introduction, exactly by the book."

Robert nodded. "Which is what he's supposed to do. That's best, at least for the side that has the better case."

"Which is us, we hope."

"Fervently."

Judge Lopez continued. Now, he was talking to the panel about avoiding jury misconduct. "And do not accept from either side any favors, no matter how small, such as rides or refreshments."

A few moments later, the judge was advising the potential jurors that the attorneys were about to ask them questions. Do not conceal information, he told them. This is how we get a fair and impartial jury.

"The attorneys now will proceed with their examinations," he said finally.

Robert stretched himself to his full height and faced the jury panel with a smile. The butterflies in his stomach disappeared as he started to speak.

* * *

"Good morning, Ladies and Gentlemen. The judge told you that I am Robert Herrick, and yes, I am. He also told you that I represent the lead plaintiff, William Grant, and yes, I do."

He gave them a wider smile and a nod, as if to acknowledge that this straightforward beginning was odd-sounding and intended to be slightly humorous. It always drew a little laugh from the jury panel. By this time, the jurors were tired of waiting and being herded around, and they were always a little leery of lawyers, and so things that wouldn't seem funny in other places drew chuckles from them, in the excessively formal atmosphere of the courtroom.

"We will show you three kinds of proofs," Robert went on. "First, the injuries to Mr. Grant were caused by the negligence of these defendants." He stretched his hand toward the defendants' table. "Second, Mr. Grant did not cause his own injuries. The defendants will be blaming him, blaming the victim, as a means to escape the results of their own carelessness. Don't fall for it." And at that, Robert wore an expression of distaste. Disgust.

"Third, we will show you that this is a very serious injury to Mr. Grant. He is unable to work, and he had a well-paying job. He has constant pain, He will require extensive medical services for the rest of his life. Even his relationship with his wife is lesser than it was."

"Is there anyone on this panel who cannot perform as a juror in a case like this?" He watched for a minute. "I take it from your silence that everyone here could do that. I didn't expect to see any hands."

Now, Robert moved to the other end of the jury bar, to signal a new subject. "Has any one of you ever worked construction? Has anyone worked in the building trades? Has any one of you worked at building tall buildings, or even short ones?"

A few jurors laughed at that. Nobody was likely to claim that they had built short buildings.

But three hands went up. Men who had worked construction.

"Mr. Flores," Robert said, speaking to the first one, "were there ever any injuries?"

"Of course."

"The equipment's dangerous if it isn't in tip-top shape, right?"

"Absolutely." Mr. Flores nodded his head. "First thing you've got to do at the job site is maintain the equipment."

Robert thought to himself, Yes! Beautiful. And he went on to the next two building tradesmen. Number two said that a crane was especially dangerous if it wasn't maintained. Number three added that you couldn't always be aware of what was happening with a crane, whether it was turning or not, because you were always in the middle of doing something. You couldn't hear everything at the job site, especially if you were at one end and someone at another end sent out a routine message that the crane was coming around.

A trial lawyer could use members of the jury panel as witnesses in favor of his case, if he did it right, Robert thought to himself. Not real "witnesses," of course, because they didn't sit at the witness stand, but the rest of the potential jurors weren't wearing earmuffs, and they heard everything their fellow panelists said. And jury panel members were the most effective kinds of "witnesses," because the rest of the jurors knew they weren't hired to help anyone's case, and in fact, they were members of the same group as the jurors.

That was what Robert was doing. Using the jurors, themselves, as witnesses.

When he finished questioning the potential jurors, he felt confident. This was a good panel.

* * *

Now it was Sammy Stubarsky's turn.

"We don't agree with Mr. Herrick," Sammy began. "In fact, we really, really disagree with him."

Sammy spread his arms over the jury panel. "Here's what this case is really about. Mr. Herrick's client—that's this guy, William Grant—had his back turned to the crane. That's a big No-No at a construction site. And he blocked the view. My clients faced the crane, but they couldn't see it. This accident was the fault of Blackminster Construction and Janowitz, yes; but there was also another person who was negligent. As negligent as all get out. And that was William Grant. He caused this accident, more than anyone else, William Grant did."

His two clients were not at fault, Sammy explained. And they were hurt badly. They should recover.

But not William Grant.

Sammy took less than five minutes to talk to the jury panel. Brevity is persuasive, sometimes; and by now, Robert Herrick was worried.

* * *

He was right to worry. Jimmy Coleman was standing, now, to speak.

"Mr. Stubarsky is correct!" he thundered. "His clients are hurt. And they weren't at fault. It will be up to you, as jurors, to figure out their damages."

Jimmy pointed. "That's William Grant. More than anyone else, he caused this accident. He's got some really tough bark on him, William Grant does, coming into this courtroom and blaming other people for the accident he caused."

The defense lawyer's pale eyes were even paler than usual, his voice even rougher, his lined face even more angry. The jury should keep in mind that a plaintiff, like William Grant, could be negligent, just like a defendant. And William Grant was negligent, for sure.

Jimmy turned to the three construction workers. From the first one, he extracted a statement that you should never turn your back on a crane. From the second, a statement that gears on cranes just tended to stick. That was what they always did, and it wasn't a big deal. The third construction guy allowed as how, yes, when people were hurt on the job, it often was their fault.

Jimmy could use members of the jury panel as witnesses, too.

In fact, when Jimmy sat down a few minutes later, Robert knew he was in trouble. He had lost whatever momentum he had built up with the jury panel in his own time for questioning. And now . . . he was losing.

* * *

Robert worked until late to get ready for tomorrow. He was exhausted when he opened the back door at home. And depressed. "Maria?" he called.

"Yes, my love."

"Don't ask me right away how it went." He wanted some cheering up. "What did you do today that was special, Baby?"

"I went to the gynecologist. And it's good news, my love. She says everything is working fine in there."

He laughed. "Okay. Good."

"And they gave me a questionnaire, which asked whether we've been having sexual relations."

"Oh, yeah?" He looked up sharply, at that.

"And I told them yes. We have sex. And Robert, another one of the questions asked . . . well . . . ah . . . how long you are, down there."

"WHAT?"

"Yes. I was surprised."

"No. They didn't really ask you that. You're pulling my chain."

"Yes. They did. And I had a hard time answering. I was taught first to use the metric system, being from Cuba. They asked in inches, and I still get confused. I had to sort of guess."

Now, he could see she was stifling a laugh.

"You really shouldn't say, 'Yes, it's true,' when I say to you, 'That didn't really happen.' You kid around too much. Some time it's going to get you in trouble."

"Sorry, Baby. But hey, I really fooled you, didn't I?"

"You sure did." He laughed too. "I guess you can fool me too easily."

"No more so than most people."

But suddenly she was serious. "Just watch out and don't get fooled in this case you're trying. You'd hate that, and so would I."

"It can happen in lawsuits, for sure. And I'm with you. I just hope it isn't happening to me in this lawsuit I'm trying for William Grant."

24

Judge Lopez's courtroom was on the nineteenth floor of the Civil Courts Building. As people tended to say, it was simple, modern, not exactly elegant, but nice. The bench was made of dark wood, set up high to emphasize the control the judge had over the courtroom. To its left, there was a witness chair, of matching wood, and beyond that, a set of fourteen jury chairs—fourteen, not twelve, so that alternate jurors could be added if the judge thought that the trial would last for a while. The chairs were all full, because neither Judge Lopez nor the lawyers could accurately predict the length of these proceedings.

The jurors were a mixture of some well-dressed men and women, and some people in casual outfits, and some just plain sloppy dressers. The phrase "rainbow coalition" has been used as a campaign device by some politicians, but as Robert Herrick looked at this group of twelve, he reflected once again upon how much more a jury fit that description—a rainbow coalition—than anything a politician might conjure up.

The walls were wood-paneled, and the floor was slightly darker, covered with a durable, nubbly carpet. The counsel tables were similar to the color of the bench. Robert Herrick, Tom Kennedy, and William and Delores Grant sat at the table nearest the jury. Sammy Stubarsky and his two clients were next.

At the other table, uncomfortably close, sat Jimmy Coleman and a man and woman from each of his client companies, plus a few members of Jimmy's black-suited entourage. There were more of those, all wearing the same uniform, sitting behind Jimmy, just in front of the bar.

Eight days of trial were about to go by in a painful blur, the way days of trial always do. Eight days of striving and arguing, without anyone knowing what is going to happen at the end, and eight nights of working most of the night to get ready for the next day.

Judge Lopez mounted to the bench, with the entire courtroom standing. "Be seated, please."

Then he turned, once again with a politican's smile because judges run for re-election in this state, toward the fourteen jurors. "Good morning, ladies and gentlemen of the jury. We will now proceed to begin this trial."

His smile continued. "But first, remember the instructions I have given you. If you don't follow these instructions"—still with a beaming smile—"we may have to erase the result of this trial and start all over. Then all of our work will have been wasted."

The judge went on, repeating standard instructions that were as familiar as the standard lines in a religious ceremony. Robert was watching the jurors closely, while they gazed at the judge with renewed attention.

Finally, the judge concluded. "The lawyers will now give their opening statements to you. Remember, what the attorneys say is not evidence. It is said to help you to organize the trial and guide your thinking, if it does. Mr. Herrick?"

This was his signal. And now he was on his feet, with the pretrial butterflies in his stomach fading away.

"Good morning, ladies and gentlemen of the jury." And they responded, nearly unanimously, with a hearty, "Good morning."

"I told you, my friends, that we would show you three themes during this trial. First, the defendants were negligent, very negligent, and their negligence injured William Grant badly." He gestured toward his client. "Second, Mr. Grant did not cause his own injuries, contrary to what the defendants will tell you. That is a cowardly argument by the defendants."

Jimmy was on his feet. "Objection, your Honor . . . !"

"Sustained," said the judge, more calmly than Jimmy. "Ladies and gentlemen, disregard that last remark of counsel."

There is a way to respond to a sustained objection that limits the damage, and Robert immediately turned to it. "Mr. Coleman is going to have his say later, ladies and gentlemen. He's going to tell you a great deal that I won't agree with, sometimes in sharp language, I predict. Now, I can have my say." He tossed off the line as a throwaway, but in clear words, as if to say, Jimmy Coleman is trying to stop me from telling you the truth.

"So, our second point is that the defendants are wrong to blame Mr. Grant for causing his own injuries. He didn't."

And now, Robert pivoted on his heel to signify a new subject, and his voice rose slightly. "Third, we will show you that it's a horrible injury, with shredded internal organs and dirty infections, that will cause pain for the rest of Mr. Grant's life, along with constant medical expenses, inability to work, and personal poverty. Damages that the law values at more than ten million dollars. And as I've told you before, dollars and cents can't ever compensate for these injuries, but it's all that the law can do, and the law says that these damages must be awarded if they are proved, and they will be."

He had done the hard part of the argument now. He paused before taking on the next part, which was to tell how his witnesses would explain each of the three points to the jury.

"You will hear from William himself. He will tell you how he came to be in Alaska. He will explain how the crane came down, far away, and swung out beyond him and then teetered back. And it bit into William's flesh just above the pelvis and traveled through the knots and spins and curves of his intestines, multiple deep cuts, until it sliced a piece of his breastbone—his sternum.

"That unexpected event, that irresponsible, bloody, terrifying event, was caused by the defendants' carelessness. And that's one small part of the proof of Theme One, that the defendants were negligent. But of course there's more proof of that—much more."

He was wound up by now, speaking passionately, even though the words here were memorized, spoken by rote. He told how the expert witnesses, witnesses who designed and used cranes, would show more about the defendant's carelessness. And he narrated the testimony of other eyewitnesses, rehabilitation experts, emergency physicians from Alaska, and doctors from here, who would give the rest of the story.

Forty-five minutes later, sweating and breathing heavily, he thanked the jurors for their attention and sat down.

* * *

Sammy Stubarsky's opening statement was breathtakingly short. Like every other appearance he had made in this case.

"Ladies and gentlemen, we disagree with Mr. Herrick. First of all, William Grant caused his own injuries. He stood with his back to the crane when it was coming down, and everyone at a construction site will tell you, firmly, you should never do that."

And then, Sammy repeated his earlier statements during jury selection. But this time he hammered them in.

"And although William Grant was the lion's share of what caused his own injuries, the defendants did have a part in it. I expect that Mr. Coleman will be honest about it, and he will tell you that Blackminster Construction and Janowitz Company were part of the cause of my clients' injuries. And you will see that those injuries, unlike Mr. Grant's, deserve to be compensated."

Robert and Tom looked at each other. It is a disadvantage, when you give a long presentation, for an opponent to deliver a pithy message in a very short presentation. It makes the opponent look much more intelligent than you seem to be.

And, of course, it was devastating to hear this message from another plaintiff, who the jury believes should be on your side.

* * *

Jimmy Coleman's opening was a little longer than Sammy's, but it was short too.

"Ladies and gentlemen, we agree with Mr. Stubarsky. His clients are truly injured. And you will see, from the cross-examination of the plaintiff's doctors and from the defendants' expert witnesses, that Mr. William Grant has grossly exaggerated his injuries. Just as he has grossly exaggerated his entire case."

Methodically, harshly, with a grating voice, but wearing a friendly smile, Jimmy attacked each of Robert Herrick's witnesses. Some were "bought and paid for, and you'll see it, not just because of the enormous sums they've been paid, but also from the contradictions they spew out." Others just hadn't seen the event the way it happened, or had the wrong facts, shaded to fit their opinions; or were "just plain biased and prejudiced."

When Jimmy sat down, Robert could see that the jurors were nowhere near where he had left them. They were skeptical of his case, now.

But there was another job to do now.

* * *

With his customary smile, Judge Lopez excused the jury. As the last of them filed into the jury room, Robert said to the judge, "Your Honor, may we be heard on a procedural matter?"

"Yes, now that the jury has been removed. Proceed."

"Your Honor, I have never seen a case in which there has been a single, unified accident injuring multiple plaintiffs, and in which one plaintiff's attorney concentrates all of his efforts against another plaintiff's attorney. But that is what has happened here. It makes no sense unless the plaintiff who attacks has made an agreement with the defendant. Your Honor, have you ever seen such a case before?"

"No. It's unusual, I admit." The judge paused. "But it depends on what the trial tactics of the plaintiff and defendant are. Is their conduct independent?"

"Exactly." Robert spat the word out with disgust. "And so I ask the other attorneys in this case: do you have an agreement, including just a silent agreement formed by your conduct, to coordinate your actions in trying this case?"

"Yes," echoed the judge. "Do you have even a tacit coordination?"

Jimmy Coleman's rasped response was immediate. "Absolutely not, your Honor."

"No," said Sammy Stubarsky, emphatically.

"Mr. Herrick is right; it's unusual." The judge shook his head. "So, why would anyone in Mr. Stubarsky's position do what he's been doing, without an agreement with the defendants?"

Again, Jimmy spoke immediately. "I imagine that Mr. Stubarsky would not want to give away his trial tactics, and neither would I. But hypothetically, there might be many reasons for a plaintiff to do what he's doing. For example, he might believe in the position he is taking—that the other plaintiff is not hurt or caused his own injuries. Or he might believe that the jury would think so, and by going along with that belief of the jury, he would increase his credibility and help his chances of winning."

"Mr. Stubarsky?" The judge sounded doubtful.

"I have no agreement with Mr. Coleman whatsoever." Sammy's voice was flat.

"I request that the court make a finding that there *is* an agreement." Robert's voice was forceful. "And I respectfully move the court to instruct the jury that those two plaintiffs have made an agreement with the defendants to oppose Mr. Grant's case and that the jurors may take that agreement into account in deciding the case."

A judge's job involves making countless decisions. Some are easy. Some are hard. And some involve suspicions of wrongdoing, in circumstances in which there is no evidence upon which to base a decision that there is wrongdoing.

There was a pause. Then, the judge ruled. "We are in recess until one o'clock. Mr. Herrick, your motion is overruled."

25

One o'clock. The judge strode up to the bench. "Mr. Herrick? Are you ready to call your first witness?"

"Your Honor, the plaintiff calls William Grant to the witness stand." Robert saw the illogic in the statement and added, "It's odd, but William Grant calls the plaintiff, who is . . . himself."

Some jurors chuckled at that, proving once again that even weak humor is appreciated in the oppressive solemnity of a courtroom. The jury watched as the plaintiff wheeled himself to the side of the witness stand and shook as he clambered into the seat.

"Tell the jury your name, please, and introduce yourself."

"William Grant. One of the plaintiffs. Together with my wife, Delores, who is seated beside you, Mr. Herrick."

"You grew up right here, in the city, William?"

"Yes, sir."

All of this had been carefully rehearsed, of course, in Robert's office. It was smooth and clear. William Grant was a good witness, intelligent enough to narrate his story but not so polished as to seem rehearsed, although he was rehearsed.

Lawyers call this the "getting to know you; getting to know all about you" part of a direct examination. Acquaint the jurors with the plaintiff. Take him through his elementary, middle and high schools, and the likelihood is that there is a juror who went to one of those schools or knows someone who did, and the witness, now, is more real to that juror.

And after Robert had taken his client through his time as a Boy Scout ("I was three merit badges short of making Eagle when I had to step down"), his college, his hobbies ("not so many since the accident"), his work history, and especially his union membership, he had the jury ready to be friends with William Grant. And then, Robert asked, "Did there come a time when you were sent to Alaska?"

Now, it was time to talk about the accident.

"Directing your attention to the day in question, William, did you have occasion to be in Alaska and on the job?"

The question would horrify English teachers, Robert knew. It started with a "dangling modifier." The "Directing" clause, they would say, doesn't modify any noun in the sentence, and that destroys the sentence structure and creates confusion. But even if it was bad English, Robert also knew, it was good rhetoric. It signaled to the witness and the jury that now he was going to start talking about the "day in question." It was designed to sound lawyerly, maybe even a little stilted, and that was why it functioned well as a signal.

Moment by moment, then, Robert led his client through the accident, his blackout, his awakening in an Alaskan hospital with terrifying pain, his wife standing by his side, his treatments that seemed to last forever, his flight back home, and his time in the hospital there.

All of that took a couple of hours, with charts, photographs, and diagrams.

Now: the plaintiff's evidence of damages.

Robert focused on the pain first. It was "always there," the plaintiff testified. It was "constant." And maybe it came in waves, yes, but it was "sharp sometimes, sharp as a knife." And then, William Grant told about his miserable experience in trying to find work in any sort of construction field, "which is the only field I know." "Nobody could hire me for anything, and I know some of them tried." And then, he told the jury about his continual hospital treatments and his awareness that these medical interventions would always be with him, like the pain.

"William." Robert stood up and sat back again, just to signal a change in subjects. "There came a time when you were a participant in a 'Day-in-the Life' film. Would you tell the jury, please, what a 'Day-in-the-Life' film is?"

"It's a movie made by someone who comes into your home. The home of someone who is injured. And the cameraman follows you all day long without saying anything, and you just do what you usually do, all day long. And the camera records it, and it can be shown to illustrate the effect of your injuries."

The Day-in-the Life film of William Grant started with the plaintiff lying in his specially designed bed, which cost $4,000. Robert directed William Grant through his narrative.

"There's a triangular, pyramid-shaped pillow to spare my stomach . . . a lot of pain to sit up, as you can see. My wife has the wheelchair, and next she is going to help me into it. A long process . . . ."

The jury seemed mesmerized. Good, Robert thought. The film showed the rest of William Grant's day. Bathing, with specific medicinal solutions in the water; dozens of pills; another pull by his wife, and another effort to steady him and get him back into the wheelchair . . . and so on, for the rest of this typical day.

"William," Robert asked at the end of the Day-in-the-Life film, "you've heard me tell this jury that it would take more than ten million dollars to compensate you for these injuries. Now, please tell the jurors the answer to this question." He paused for dramatic effect. "Would you, William, if you had the chance, accept ten million dollars to suffer through the life that you now have, or William, would you give up the ten million and keep the life you had before?"

The injured man's eyes glistened. He swallowed hard, and his eyes became even more glazed, and finally, wet. "With medical procedures forever, not being able to work, not doing anything that used to be fun, not being able to relate to my wife as a wife, depending on her to lift me with her back, and being in constant pain, there's . . . no . . . question. I think I deserve to recover against these careless defendants. But I'd certainly give it all up for my life before."

His voice caught. "I'd . . . give up . . . ten million dollars. Or ten billion, or ten trillion."

"Pass the witness," said Robert, with the jury still staring, some of them open-mouthed, at the plaintiff.

"That went all right," he whispered to Tom Kennedy. But as they both knew, Jimmy Coleman's cross-examination was coming next.

* * *

Everybody was surprised when Sammy Stubarsky said, "No questions." Maybe he decided he had repeated himself too often already, Robert thought.

"Mr. Coleman?" the judge said quietly.

"Good afternoon, Mr. Grant," the grinding voice announced.

"Ahhh . . . Good . . . Afternoon."

Jimmy got right into it. "When a crane comes around at a construction site, it is announced loudly, isn't it, Mr. Grant?"

"Ahhh . . . yes." The plaintiff had just loosed all of his emotions. Now, facing Jimmy Coleman, he was already confused and nervous, with the cross-examination barely underway. He trembled. Everyone in the courtroom could see it.

Jimmy didn't notice. "And everyone pays attention when the crane comes around, don't they?"

"Yes . . . ."

"But you didn't."

"I was facing away."

"Which was careless, wasn't it?"

"I don't . . . I don't . . . think I was . . . careless."

"Let me read your deposition, your sworn testimony before this trial," Jimmy thundered. "I asked you, 'And if you hadn't turned your back, you could have seen the hook, and nothing would have happened, right?' And your answer was, 'Ahhh . . . I guess so.'"

"And then I asked, 'You were contributorily negligent yourself, weren't you?' And I asked, 'Turning your back was a careless thing, wasn't it?' And you answered, 'I guess so.' You said all of that, didn't you, Mr. Grant, and admitted that you were negligent?"

"If you say so."

"And at that time, you were under oath, just like here?"

"Yes."

"You told me you knew what a deposition was, and you knew it could be read back to you if you told a different story at trial. You knew all of that?"

"Yes."

"At the deposition, under oath, after you had raised your hand and sworn, you knew you had to get it right. You knew that if you ever were going to get it right, you needed to get it right, at that moment, in this deposition. Didn't you?"

"I guess so . . . ."

"And so, we can take your sworn statement for it that you made then. You were careless. You were contributorily negligent."

It wasn't a question. Robert shifted, involuntarily, uncomfortably, in his chair. Tom Kennedy was nervously twisting a rubber band, then loosening it slowly, again and again. Delores Grant had her mouth open and her hand raised over her neck, and she looked ready to cry out as she stared at her husband, helpless to make his situation any better.

The cross-examination went on, this way, for a solid hour, not counting a recess that Judge Lopez spontaneously granted for William Grant to get some water. Robert hoped that William would be a better witness after the recess.

He wasn't.

We're losing this case, Robert thought, when the cross–examination ended, and the plaintiff's wife finally came to help him, delicately, shakily, to get down from the witness stand to the wheelchair.

26

The trial slowly ground into day four.

The testimony of William Grant was a distant memory by now. It would be Robert Herrick's job, later, to ensure that its better parts were a present memory, and a forceful one, for the jury.

Billy Broadhurst's testimony had followed immediately after William Grant's. Billy, the second plaintiff, was a distant memory too, but Robert remembered Billy all too vividly.

Sammy Stubarsky had taken his client through the accident in a way that did not resemble William Grant's testimony. When he asked Billy Broadhurst about the crane, Billy put the fault squarely on William.

"Could you see the crane moving, Billy?"

"No. Willie Grant was uphill from us, and we were standing in a depression. And Willie Grant is big. And tall. The view was blocked."

"Could you hear anything?"

"If I'd been where Willie was standing, I think I could have. But I couldn't. Willie was talking to us, and he was loud."

"And so, Willie's negligence caused this accident?"

Robert had stood immediately. "Objection, your Honor. That calls for an opinion that a witness like this one cannot properly give. And Mr. Stubarsky knows it."

"Sustained," the judge had said. But the question had been heard, by everyone, including the jury, and it summed up what Billy was saying.

Then there were the witnesses who had been nearer the crane. Including the crane operator. But those witnesses weren't as impressive as the three who had stood together when the crane hit them.

Even the crane operator didn't seem to make the accident sound so much the fault of the crane company or Blackminster Construction. He was inexperienced, yes, but he testified that the gears on the crane were not a significant problem. And this young man had a certain charm, the charm of the brash and inexperienced. Jury sympathy for the careless crane operator would help to protect his employers, the defendants—because it's usually not a sin, or at least it's not a bad one, to hire a young man who has charm. To give a new employee a chance.

Now, it was time for Robert's expert witness, to talk about how the crane should have been operated.

"Please tell the jury your name and your qualifications," he asked.

"I'm Caleb McDonald. Worked for thirty years with cranes, first with selling them, meaning you have to know all about them. Then, operating them. Then, supervising and teaching about them." McDonald told about his work in continuing education programs, designed to keep crane operators up to date.

"Please tell us about this crane."

"It was a Liebherr 550 HCC model, a good, reliable crane. In use everywhere."

"Tell us how it works, please, Mr. McDonald."

"There are two toggle switches, one for turning and braking on the left, and one to control the trolley on the right. Most of the operation of the boom and trolley is done by these. There are floor-mounted controls that raise and lower the cab. And that's the controls you most have to understand, although there are many, many others, and indicators, that are used for all kinds of things."

"You mentioned a 'trolley.' What's that?"

"Oh, I'm sorry." The witness was an old hand with juries, and he smiled as he looked at the citizens. "The trolley is the mechanism that travels out and in on the boom. Its pulleys and lines connect to the load. At the time, I understand, the trolley was carrying rebar up to the second floor pad." He paused, then added quickly, "Rebar is steel bars that are used to reinforce and form the concrete that builds the building."

"What difficulties might a brand new crane operator experience in operating this kind of crane on a windy day? Is it harder, than—say— driving a car for the first time?"

"Much harder. First of all, you're way up high. So high that a lot of people can't do it, because it feels like you're about to fall any minute. If you're afraid of heights or being on the edge of a cliff, you can't do it. Second, there's more controls. A lot more. Third, they are slow to respond. When you turn, it takes time; when you stop, it takes time. And the time it takes is unpredictable, because it depends on the sharpness of the controls, the operator's wrist, the trolley grease, the boom length, and the wind. The boom length is 265 feet on this machine, and so it's like driving a car that's nearly a football field away. And then there's the wind. It was really windy this day. Your crane, hook, and load can all be swaying like the dickens."

"Would it be prudent, or careful, for an inexperienced operator to operate this crane on this day?"

"Absolutely not. This would have been a job for a very experienced operator. The load could sway at a nearly thirty degree arc at times, fifteen degrees each side. And I might add that the way the crane was maintained wasn't prudent, or careful, either."

* * *

But Jimmy's cross-examination took away a great deal of what the expert had said.

"A new crane operator doesn't just become experienced without operating, does he?"

"No. A new operator gets experience from operating. You've got to start somewhere, and I guess this guy was starting."

"And wind comes and goes, doesn't it? You can't ever really predict it?"

"You can predict, but a lot of the time you'll be wrong."

"This new operator had been through all the usual training, and he was certified to operate this model crane, right?"

"Yes. I guess so."

"So, a construction supervisor might very well consider all of that, and then, might decide to have this operator do what he was trained to do?"

"I suppose so. I wouldn't have, but someone might disagree."

I thought we were ahead, Robert said to himself. But it's clear we're not. In fact, as of now, we're behind.

* * *

Robert called another longtime crane operator like Caleb McDonald, but this time, the focus was upon jobsite safety. This expert witness testified that the accident should have been avoided by greater safety precautions on the part of the defendants.

But later, Robert knew, during the defendants' part of the case, Jimmy would be calling an expert who would testify to the precise opposite: the defendants had operated the crane in a safe manner, it was a freak occurrence, and these three plaintiffs were injured in an unavoidable accident. And Jimmy's expert would say that no one, not even a more talented crane operator, could have anticipated the overswing of the crane hook that occurred. Robert knew because he had taken that expert's deposition.

The jurors' heads would be spinning, no doubt, at the contradictions. But now, there was nothing to do but go forward with the plaintiff's case.

"Call your next," said the judge.

Robert's next expert came to tell the jury about construction management. The expert said that the placement of the crane with respect to the other structures on the site made it too likely that the crane would spin out of control.

"There were high power lines in the swing path of the crane?"

"Yes. And usually, that is avoidable."

"How?"

"Simply by repositioning the crane so that it doesn't travel across the power lines. This may require some positioning and repositioning, and sometimes engineers try to keep from having to do that extra effort, by leaving the crane in a dangerous place. That's lazy, but it's what happened here."

"What problems do those cause, the power lines?"

"You have to lift the load above the power wires and then, when you're past the power lines, let it back down. There are several problems caused by that. The wind changes. It may be stronger, and the load sways more. The lift has to be precise. And it makes for more trouble in dropping the load. An experienced operator using a well-maintained crane can do it, but I understand that this was a poorly maintained crane and a rookie operator."

But then, Jimmy got the expert to contradict that testimony, by saying that construction sites are always crowded, and this one was more neatly arranged than most.

"There was another crane on the other side that could have tangled with this one?" Jimmy asked.

"Well, yes," the expert conceded. "Another crane on another job. And that would have been a disaster, if they had collided."

As Robert and Tom left the courtroom that day, it was hard not to be discouraged. "It's like one step forward and two steps back."

Tom shook his head. "Yes, and we can only wonder what the jury thinks of it."

* * *

On the fourth day, after the construction safety expert testified, Robert came home early, at ten o'clock at night. He would have a day away from trial tomorrow, and he would work on preparing the rest of the trial. Maria got out a bottle of Talisker for him.

"A Scotch from the Isle of Skye," she said, with a contrived sort of cheerfulness, but cheerfulness nonetheless.

"Do you think I ought to be drinking that? Even if I'm not in trial tomorrow, I'll have a hard day, getting ready to argue with Jimmy and present the other expert witnesses, such as the doctors. And I'd better start preparing my final argument."

"One will be fine. Don't worry. Just pretend that I'm your athletic trainer, only I'm training you to relax and work tomorrow."

He smiled. "All right."

And a half hour later, Maria had poured him a second one with just a little soda, and she was saying, "Only one more. Now, I'm not just your trainer, I'm the enforcer too."

But she was interrupted by a series of loud bangs that shook the house.

"Gunshots," said Robert. He got his AR-15 from the hallway—it was there because of earlier cases that had brought earlier threats, other assaults, and previous drive-by shootings—and told Maria to stay in the kitchen, down. He called the nearby police officer that Detectives Slaughter and Cashdollar had arranged. And he went out the back door, slid across the side of the house, crouched by the fence, and looked out on the street.

There was nothing.

He waited. A few minutes later, the officer arrived, with the gumball machine on top of his car flashing. Then there was a second officer, and then a third.

There was nothing. And then Robert saw it.

The tires were flat on Robbie's car: Robert Junior's car. All four tires. So that was what the gunshots were about. He walked around the car. There was a brick lying on top of the hood. It had dented the metal. It had a big square of cardboard stuck to it. Glued to it.

"Don't touch it," said one of the officers.

But everyone could read the words on the cardboard. "Next time, worse," it said in hand-printed capitals. The letters were oddly formed, as though one person had written half of each one and another had finished each letter. It was a way to avoid creating any traceable handwriting.

He knew what it meant. Settle the case. And make the possibility of losing union jobs go away.

It took about an hour to brief the officers. A gloved policeman removed the cardboard sign, still attached to the brick, to deposit it at the Police Property Room. The officers found three .44 caliber bullet shells, which would go to the same place.

"Whoever did it is long gone," Robert said. The officers nodded.

It was after midnight.

"Well, I imagine you're a little less relaxed now," Maria said. She was still struggling to sound cheerful. "But go to bed. You've got to work hard tomorrow."

27

Threat or no threat, shooting or no shooting, the trial of William Grant's claim was going to continue. Detectives Slaughter and Cashdollar had come, once again, to visit Robert, and they said they had arranged to keep the nearby officer even more vigilant.

"He's gonna be on a hair trigger alert," Cashdollar pronounced. And that was the best that could be done.

If you try a lot of cases, you get used to trying some of them with distractions hanging over you, from both personal and business problems. Robert met Tom at the courthouse and avoided talking about the subject.

Today was the day to present the medical witnesses and the labor economist. With the trial underway, and a physician on the witness stand, Robert got down to business and forgot last night.

"Doctor Hulsey, you were a treating physician for William Grant here at Methodist Hospital?"

"Yes."

"Please describe his injuries, in words as close to laymen's terms as you can."

"He presented in a most unusual manner, although he had been treated at an Anchorage Hospital before he came to us. It was a latitudinal, meaning vertical, blunt trauma and incision, closed in Anchorage, from below the umbilicus to the sternum. There was extensive damage to structures underneath, including the peritoneum—the covering—and the intestines, both large and small, as well as the liver and pancreas."

"What was the treatment?"

"The teams in Anchorage had done a good job. We opened the abdomen with a midline incision, following the original trauma. It's called a linea alba incision. We cut the peritoneum with the usual scissors method. The patched and sutured parts were rough and healing. We went about the business of reconstruction and resection."

"Will you please tell the jury what reconstruction and resection mean?"

"The original injury had tangled and minced the small intestines, especially. It was necessary to suture those parts that could be reattached. That is reconstruction. In some instances, there is a need to resection, that is, to cut out a portion of intestine to reconnect, when it is so ragged and unmatched that the ends do not fit together."

"How much was Mr. Grant's intestine shortened?"

"It is not possible to be precise, because there were so many resections and so many stretched parts, traumatically injured pieces with need to resection, but I'd say, at least a total of six inches, more or less."

"Doctor, by way of comparison, there are seat belt injuries from automobile accidents. How would Mr. Grant's injuries differ from those?"

"There is literally no comparison, other than to say that this was much worse. In a car wreck, a seat belt exerts a disproportionate force on the abdomen and can cause internal trauma. If there is no internal bleeding, seat belt injuries can usually be addressed without incision or laporotomy. Ahh, excuse me, by the word laporotomy, I meant 'without opening the abdomen completely by a wide incision,' to speak in laymen's terms."

"Doctor, will Mr. Grant be vulnerable to infection, and what will this mean to him in terms of movement and pain?"

"Infection is always an ongoing concern. Movement causes pain, and infection magnifies the pain tenfold."

Dr. Hulsey's direct testimony lasted over two hours. It reached its highest drama when the doctor identified and explained photographs of the original surgery in Alaska and the surgeries he performed. To lay people, these pictures were gross and disturbing, and the discomfort of the jurors registered on their faces.

Jimmy Coleman offered only a short cross-examination, suggesting ambiguities in the doctor's testimony that might mean a less severe injury. And he asked about his own doctor.

"Dr. Hulsey, you know Dr. Alan Wecshoff, don't you?"

"Of course."

"I predict that Dr. Wecshoff will disagree with some of your conclusions when he testifies later in this case. Does that surprise you?"

Dr. Hulsey smiled. "No. I doubt there's ever any injury, this complicated, about which physicians wouldn't have any disagreement."

We got through that pretty well, Robert thought.

"Call your next," said the judge.

"The plaintiffs call Professor Thomas H. Xavier, your Honor, who is a labor economist."

Professor Xavier was here, he explained, to talk to the jury about the economic losses suffered by William Grant. The injured man was unlikely to be able to do any kind of work at a construction site, of course. And that was his line of work, the work he knew. He could perhaps find other employment, but it would be difficult to find much beyond minimum wage, because Mr. Grant's injuries would prevent him from any kind of steady operations, require too-frequent breaks, and cause unpredictable pain.

"Professor, what amount do you believe Mr. Grant could have earned," Robert asked, "if he had not been injured, and if he had continued progressing at his job?"

"My calculations show that he would have been able to earn more than three million dollars, which are a total loss."

"Would you explain the ingredients of those calculations, Professor?"

"Surely. I considered Mr. Grant's earnings over his employment history. In the building trades, salaries and bonuses tend to continue the same trajectory over time. He earned just over Two Hundred and Fifty Thousand dollars in his last full year of work. There is good reason to believe that this amount would increase to Five Hundred Thousand over the next five years, given his earnings history. He had a working life of at least ten more years."

Professor Xavier faced the jurors. "Adding the earnings with periodic increases over that time, and discounting the total to present value, I reached a result of more than three million dollars."

Jimmy's cross-examination began with a snarl. "Of course, Mr. Xavier, your prediction that Mr. Grant would earn all that money within five years is just a hopeful guess, isn't it? In fact, it's like pie in the sky?"

"No!" The witness was taken aback. "It's an estimate, sure. It's a prediction, sure. But some predictions are good ones. For example, I can predict that the sunrise will be in the east tomorrow."

"It might turn out to be whole lot less, mightn't it, Mr. Xavier?" Jimmy carefully avoided calling the witness by the honorific 'Professor.'"

"It could. That's the nature of predictions. But a whole lot less? It's possible, but I'd say it's not likely."

When Robert rested his case, he remembered the same thought that he and Tom had repeated before this trial began. "Nothing's ever easy."

* * *

Jimmy Coleman started his case for the defense the next morning, and he made sure it started with a bang.

"Dr. Williams," Jimmy asked his expert witness, "you've spent a lifetime studying and teaching about workplace safety. Do you consider the crane that you examined, the one used in this case, to be unsafe?"

"No. The toggle switches worked fine. The lines to the trolley and to the load were working as they should. Every crane requires operating skills, especially in the wind, but this one was no more difficult than others, and better than some."

And the rest of Jimmy's case was smooth, too. A labor economist to contradict Robert's economist. An experienced crane operator to contradict the testimony about the inexperienced operator in this case. An eyewitness, whom Robert hadn't called to testify, who said that the wind picked up the trolley wires in a way that just was unpredictable. An unavoidable accident.

For Robert and Tom, who took turns cross-examining, it all went by in a blur. They made some points. But as they thought about it, was it all enough?

28

After both sides rested, Judge Lopez ordered a recess for a day. It was a welcome intervention. But the next morning, at eleven o'clock, the trial resumed. And a few minutes after that, Robert was deeply into it again, giving his opening argument to the jury.

He knew, from many trials, to keep the opening argument calm and quiet. He would get another chance to speak to the jury, after the defendants finished. His opening consisted mainly of going over the questions that the jury would have to answer and building the evidence that would answer them.

"Remember, negligence just means carelessness. And these defendants were careless in so many ways. Using a crane that didn't work right. Using a crane operator who didn't know what he was doing, to handle the crane that didn't work right." And, of course, the defendants were responsible for that crane operator's carelessness, too. "The crane swung out way too far when it turned, and the expert witnesses told you that this was negligence, too."

He pointed at the defendants' table as he said, "The evidence and the law are both telling you the same thing. I ask you, I beg you . . . answer this question according to the law and the evidence. Blackminster Construction and Janowitz Company were both negligent."

After forty-five minutes, he sat down. He reserved another forty-five minutes for rebuttal, at the end.

Sammy Stubarsky, as usual, took only a few minutes. But almost all of it involved denunciation of Robert's argument to the jury. "The correct answer isn't what Mr. Herrick has told you. His client was negligent. If negligence were electricity, William Grant would be a powerhouse. And he isn't hurt."

But Sammy's clients were badly hurt, according to him. And they deserved big damages. "At least five hundred thousand dollars to each of them."

Jimmy Coleman gave an argument that surprised Robert. "William Grant's case is just an effort to get revenge from a company that he never liked, because he's not working anymore."

And Jimmy had a great deal of backup for deploring this, about how bad it was to seek revenge. "Plato said how cruel it was to seek revenge. So did St. Paul. And then, there was Beccaria . . . ."

As one courtroom observer put it, "Jimmy Coleman went on and on, quoting philosophers and guys like Beccaria, that I never heard of. All about how bad it was to get revenge. I'm not sure what it had to do with anything, but it sure did sound good."

And Jimmy agreed that Sammy Stubarsky's clients were hurt, "about as bad as he says." But William Grant wasn't hurt at all.

When Robert stood to give his final argument, his rebuttal argument, the courtroom was silent. "I have nothing personal against Mr. Coleman. But you can see, he's just doing what he hired on to do. Defending his clients, no matter what the evidence is."

He pointed out two things Jimmy had misstated about the evidence, but only two. He didn't want to let Jimmy control where his own argument was going. And then he went over the questions, but hitting the high points. "Percentages of negligence? Fifty percent to Blackminster Construction, for supplying a defective crane, and fifty percent to Janowitz, for hiring an operator who wasn't qualified. If both of them hadn't been negligent, together, this tragedy wouldn't have happened."

And by now, his voice was rising. He went into his conclusion, about how important it was for the jury to do its job.

"You know, you're twelve people, but you represent all of this city. All of this county. I wish there were glass all around, and a loudspeaker, so that everyone could see the justice that results from this case.

". . . Because you, the jurors, are the last link in the chain that supports the law. The law that we all depend on. I can do my job. The witnesses can tell you the truth. And the judge can work hard, as

Judge Lopez does. But it doesn't matter at all, if there's not a jury to follow the evidence and the law. That's up to you."

His voice rose a notch farther. "William Grant is hurt badly. You've seen the photographs of his injuries from the time. You've seen how he was patched together. You've heard what the doctors said about the destruction of his small and large intestines, and what it will mean to him for the rest of his life. No work. No activities that require running or driving or even walking. Constant pain."

He pointed at the defendants and said, "And these defendants have the gall to say he's not hurt! He's got constant pain and will have for the rest of his life. Imagine, please, that you're given fifty million dollars, but you're told: 'You can only get these millions if you'll agree to live in constant pain, hour by hour, minute by minute. You can buy a mansion in River Oaks, and a yacht, but you've got to enjoy it all with constant pain.'"

He paused. "None of you would take that deal. And that's why the least possible amount for damages for William Grant is ten million dollars."

His last words were just above a whisper. "I can't do it myself. You can. I need your help."

He sat down, heavily. Exhausted.

* * *

The jurors were out for five hours. Then they sounded the buzzer. There weren't many questions that they had to answer, compared to some cases.

"I'm not sure of this case at all," said Robert.

"Neither am I," said Tom. "It started with the other plaintiffs' lawyers acting like they were defense lawyers, in the way they struck the jurors."

"And it continued all the way through."

The jurors shuffled in, slowly. They avoided looking at the plaintiff.

"I bet the defendants and the other plaintiffs had one of those no-deal deals," Robert whispered to Tom.

When he was handed the verdict papers, the judge took what seemed like forever studying them. Finally, looking puzzled, he said, "The . . . verdict seems to be in order."

He read the jury's answers then, aloud. Blackminster Construction and Janowitz Company were each twenty percent negligent. But William Grant was sixty percent at fault.

Sammy Stubarsky's clients recovered five hundred thousand dollars each. William Grant recovered . . . nothing.

Jimmy Coleman was so happy he was almost dancing. A Booker and Bayne associate stage-whispered, "We did it!"

As he left the courtroom, Jimmy walked behind Robert. "Herrick, looks like you brought a piece-of-shit case to the courthouse."

And the black-suited Booker and Bayne associates all giggled at that.

29

Like almost every lawyer, Robert Herrick went through times when he drank too much. This was one of those times.

He kept a bar in the corner of his office. Ordinarily, he didn't think about it much. Today, he had come to the office with the best of intentions: to work on upcoming cases. But after he'd tried for fifteen minutes to concentrate on a lawsuit about a deal that had gone wrong, he gave up and wandered to the corner of the room.

It was a choice between Talisker and Glenfarclas. Two north-country Scotches. He lifted both bottles. Finally, he poured Glenfarclas over ice and added a little water.

Two hours later, he was heavily buzzed. Tom Kennedy came into the office and started drinking Glenfarclas too.

"We lost." That was Tom's pronouncement.

"Ah . . . yeah." Robert didn't really want to talk about it. "And our client has tried to kill himself, which makes it even worse."

Tom took the hint. And both of them were silent until the intercom buzzed

"Robert, I know you didn't want to be disturbed," said Donna deCarlo. "But I think you'll want to take this call."

"Oh? What makes you think that?" He didn't want to take anybody's call.

"It's about William Grant's case. The *William Grant v. Blackminster Construction* case. And it's the bailiff from the courtroom."

Donna deCarlo's voice rose. "He says he heard Sammy Stubarsky and Jimmy Coleman talking. Right before the jury selection. Making a deal about the jury."

Robert was foggy enough at this point to want to say, "I'll call him back." But through the whiskey fog, he realized, in spite of himself, that he'd better . . . take . . . this particular call.

Laboriously, he picked up the phone receiver.

Slowly, he put it to his ear.

It took a few seconds before he was able to force himself to say, "Hello?"

The voice on the other end of the line was precise. Almost military. "Mr. Herrick, this is Sergeant Rodriguez from the sheriff's department. I'm the bailiff in Judge Lopez's court."

"Yes, sir. What can I do for you?" Robert had to suppress a burp. "Hold on, please." He held the receiver at arm's length.

"I've been thinking about talking to you for a long time," said the sergeant. "It may be nothing."

"Yes?"

"I saw something unusual. It was right before all of you lawyers put in your jury strikes to select the jury. You know, for that case involving the crane that hurt the guy. Anyway, right beforehand, Mr. Stubarsky and Mr. Coleman were standing there in the back hallway, you know, between the jury room and the judge's chambers."

A pause. "Yes?" said Robert, again.

Then, he said, "I've got my partner Tom here with me. The one who tried the case with me. If it's okay, I'm going to put you on the speaker so he can hear too."

Tom had had a little less to drink.

"Okay," said the sergeant. "So. These two lawyers, or one of them anyways, said something about the jury, and something about numbers. And Mr. Coleman gave Mr. Stubarsky one of those little sticky squares of paper. I couldn't hear it very well, and I couldn't see much about what was on the paper. But there was writing."

Now, Robert was alert, even if it was a hazy kind of alert. "Yes?" he said again, a little more assertively this time.

"Well, I know there was this big issue about whether those two lawyers had an agreement to work together. If there was an agreement between lawyers on opposite sides during a trial, you had a right to know about it, of course."

"Yes!"

"So, I heard these two gentlemen a few minutes later tell the judge that they didn't have no agreement. And I thought it was fishy. What was all a that, then, that was going on between the two of them in the hallway, with the yellow stickie?"

Robert waited.

"And I was right well surprised when they told the judge they didn't have no sort of agreement, because it sure looked like they was putting on agreement together there in the back hallway. Almost like Louisiana, where they make crooked deals behind the barnyard."

"They didn't say anything about agreeing, when they passed the yellow stickie?"

"Not that I heard."

"But it looked like an agreement?"

"It looked like they was planning to do something together, and I didn't figure they had plans to go to lunch."

"You've testified in court before, Sergeant?"

"It's been a while, but yes, several times. I don't arrest nobody no more. And here in the courtroom, I don't see too many crimes being committed."

"I don't suppose so."

"'Less'n you count perjury, that is."

"Right."

"So, I been thinking about talking to you for a while because I thought you ought to know."

"Yes, sir. You've done the right thing, Sergeant Rodriguez. And I appreciate it. My client appreciates it."

"Yeah. The guy was hurt."

"We will take action on this, Sergeant. We will file a Motion for New Trial. At the very least.

"The judge will hear about it."

* * *

It took a few minutes before either Robert or Tom said anything. Robert looked at the multicolor diamond shapes on the carpet, and then out the tall windows past the green of Memorial Park, to the horizon—and studied it. Tom was looking at the tiny cars, so many stories down, that were creeping along the freeways.

"Tomorrow," said Robert, finally. "Tomorrow."

"Right. We're in no shape to do it today."

"Tomorrow," Robert said again, unnecessarily.

"I'll come in early and get started on a Motion for New Trial."

They both had another glass of very good whiskey. And Robert called Maria, who diagnosed the situation immediately. "I'll come get you. You're worthwhile most of the time, even if you don't sound like it right now."

30

"This Motion for New Trial is pretty unusual." Tom Kennedy sat at one of the three mahogany-and-leather chairs in Robert's office. Outside, the rain beat against the floor-to-ceiling windows, almost obscuring the greensward of Buffalo Bayou that swept toward the mist where the horizon would usually be.

Robert grinned. "It's an unusual situation, so the Motion ought to be a little different." Beneath him, the magnificent carpet with its riotous colors stretched toward a hundred geraniums in red and pink.

The heading was standard, but the Motion made a serious charge.

<u>No. 16-1718</u>

William Grant et ux.,	**In the District Court**
Plaintiffs	
v.	**No. 285 of Harris**
Blackminster Construction, et al.,	**County, TX**
Defendants	

PLAINTIFF GRANT'S MOTION FOR NEW TRIAL

Plaintiffs William and Delores Grant would respectfully show the Court as follows, in a hearing at which evidence will be submitted:

1. Attorneys for Defendants Blackminster and Janowitz were asked before trial whether they had made an agreement to coordinate their conduct of the trial. They assured the Honorable Judge in open Court that they had reached no agreement to combine or otherwise work together in concert to oppose any

recovery by Plaintiff William Grant or to assure a recovery by the other two Plaintiffs.

2. Their conduct throughout the trial showed, instead, that exactly such an agreement existed.

3. The meaning of Defendants' assurances was apparently that they did not communicate any such agreement by words. Instead, they both agreed silently to engage in parallel behavior during the trial. Nevertheless, an agreement existed.

4. New evidence has come to light after trial, that Plaintiff Grant and his attorneys could not have known about even with the greatest amount of diligence, to prove the existence of this agreement . . . .

Robert studied the Motion. He wanted it to send a message: a wakeup call. It should frankly say what the defense lawyers had done wrong, he thought. At the same time, he wanted to avoid exaggeration. He didn't think it should contain an outright accusation of fraud on the court.

Tom's document struck just the right tone. The accusation was there, but it emerged from the facts that were stated, not from overheated rhetoric. After a moment, he picked up a pen from a carved marble desk holder, a gift from a grateful client. Wordlessly, he signed the Motion for New Trial.

Then: "Good. File it."

* * *

A few days later, the same two sometime adversaries who had come together earlier met again with a common purpose.

The setting, again, was the magnificent main bar at the River Oaks Country Club. Gunther Blackminster was a big man with sandy hair who wore a charcoal pinstriped suit. The little, unkempt fellow across the table from him sported a green plaid jacket with a gray tie. The founder and president of Blackminster Construction Company was eager to talk to the union president.

"We got a good result in that trial," The big man said. "It looked good. That Jimmy Coleman did a fantastic job for us."

"No question about it. So what's the problem now?"

"William Grant's lawyers have filed something called a Motion for New Trial. That's a lawyer thing that asks the judge to throw out the jury verdict and start all over."

"I didn't know a judge can do that."

"Mr. Coleman assures me that he can."

"Is it gonna happen?"

"Nobody knows. Mr. Coleman seems confident. But hey, he always seems confident. He looks worried about it to me."

"What does that mean?"

"After we won the trial, I told you we had won everything we needed to win. We didn't need to try any farther to persuade Mr. Herrick to lay off. To settle the case for something that we at Blackminster Construction could afford to pay without losing jobs and laying people off."

"Right. Let's not have any of that."

"Well, now the problem's come back again. Full force. Maybe even worse. It's like what you see in the movies. The bad guy is dead, but then he stands up and still wants to kill you. The Creature from the Black Lagoon rises out of the water and attacks."

The union man laughed at that. But immediately he stopped laughing. It wasn't a laughing matter.

"We could use the union's help again. To persuade this lawyer."

"I figured that out, even before the Black Lagoon thing."

"I don't want to know about it."

"No problem. We'll get the word out."

Gunther Blackminster called for the check and signed his name.

31

Jimmy Coleman stared out the window at the city, not seeing the buildings, not seeing the cars that inched along the freeways dozens of floors below. "Jennifer, we've got a problem with this Motion for New Trial that Robert Herrick has filed."

Jennifer Lowenstein sat opposite Jimmy's honey-colored desk, with its inlays of vines and flowers that matched the priceless Italian chest next to her. "Why is that, Jimmy? Herrick claims you had a deal, an agreement, with Sammy Stubarsky. To gang up on his client, and to favor Sammy's clients. But you didn't have an agreement."

"Well, but it's all in how you interpret it."

"How so?"

"What is an 'agreement'? Is it explicit, with spoken or written words? Or is it a mutual understanding?"

"I'd say it means there's some kind of communication. Which you didn't have."

"Yes. But that, Jennifer, depends on what you mean by communication."

"You're being too much like a lawyer for me." She laughed. "Too subtle. It sounds like, 'Hey, it depends on what the meaning of *is* is.'"

"I suppose so. And, of course, that's what we'll argue to the judge. We told the judge we didn't have an 'agreement' with Sammy Stubarsky. What we meant, was that we didn't exchange any *words* of agreement. And to us, that's what an agreement is. Robert Herrick is going to answer that argument by saying we had an agreement without words, by silence, by an understanding that depends on a wink and a nod."

"Well, but you didn't have a wink and a nod, either. Did you?"

"No. But you understand what I mean. And so will the judge. Manny Lopez is no dummy. He'll see what Herrick is arguing. An agreement by silence, that both parties formed by their actions."

"I'd call that trial strategy. Just plain old trial strategy."

"And you'd argue, of course, that both we and Sammy figured out that our best trial strategy was to blame Herrick's client. To blame William Grant. And so, you'd say, we independently adopted strategies that, on our side, meant arguing that William Grant got nothing while Sammy's clients got overpaid, because from our standpoint, we saved money by not owing anything to Grant. And on Sammy's side, his independent strategy meant that his clients received more, without a real fight."

"Exactly. It's trial strategy."

"But there's another way to see it. Are these strategies really independent? The success of our strategy of saving money by paying Sammy's clients and not paying the big one, William Grant—that strategy depended on our knowing that Sammy would also follow that strategy, by attacking William Grant."

"I guess. But it's still trial strategy. And you didn't have an agreement as I'd define it, because you didn't exchange words of agreement."

"Well, that's certainly going to be our position."

"Isn't it a winning position? So, no problem?"

"That depends on whether Herrick can get across his argument that even without words, still, there was a silent agreement. And we didn't disclose it."

"And if the judge thinks Herrick's right about that . . . ."

". . . then he's likely to give Herrick a new trial and wipe out our victory. As I said, Judge Manny Lopez is no dummy."

"So, that's why you say we have a problem."

"Yes. But we do have one big advantage."

"What's that?"

"How can Herrick prove what we were thinking?" Jimmy smiled. "The answer is, it won't be easy. And we can deny, deny, deny that we had an agreement, without lying, because according to our definition of what an agreement is, we didn't."

* * *

"So, Tom. We've charged that the Defendants had an agreement and didn't tell the truth to the judge at the start of trial. That's what we've said in the Motion for New Trial. But how do we *prove* it?"

"We call the bailiff to the witness stand to testify that Jimmy Coleman gave Sammy Stubarsky a yellow square stickie in the back hallway. And that's how they agreed to their strategy during the jury selection. Sammy struck some extra potential jurors that Jimmy wanted to remove."

The sun washed over the floor-to-ceiling windows in Robert's office. The day was full of blue skies, and the greenery of Buffalo Bayou and Memorial Park stretched out to the horizon. To the south, the spires of the city poked upward in tones of brown, beige, and white.

"Well, that would help Jimmy, for sure. If you give me a few extra jurors that are favorable to me, I can win the case most of the time just because of that. And I can do it if someone like Sammy Stubarsky lets me remove a few extra ones that I don't want."

"Okay. So, it's not a perfect proof, but maybe it's enough."

"Well, but here's the problem. We don't know what was on the yellow square stickie. And the bailiff doesn't know. So we'd have trouble proving it by that."

"And then, we can point to the trial transcript itself. Sammy did, in fact, remove potential jurors that he shouldn't have wanted to remove, as a plaintiff. He gave a very strange opening statement that blamed a fellow plaintiff. His questioning throughout was about proving that William Grant was negligent, and his final arguments to the jury were a denunciation of his fellow plaintiff, Grant, instead of against the defendants."

"And that gets us closer."

"What else?"

"Two things." Robert stared out the window toward the distant horizon. "First, we get an expert witness who can say that these facts amounted to an agreement."

"And that would be . . . ."

"My old professor. Professor Perry Jones. Famous across the state. The Father of Tort Reform."

"Okay." Tom smiled for the first time. "And the second thing?"

"We take the depositions of Jimmy Coleman and Sammy Stubarsky. They'll do their best to avoid our questions, of course. But they can't avoid them completely. They'll be saying, 'That's my trial strategy, so it's privileged and I don't have to answer about it.' And for some questions—the 'What were you thinking at the time?' kind of questions—it will, in fact be trial strategy, and we can't get it."

"But if we ask what they *did* together . . . ."

"Exactly. What you did in cooperation with an adversary in trial isn't strategy. It's conduct. And it's fair game for questions."

"And of course, it might show that you had an agreement with that adversary for a joint presentation of the case." Tom smiled too.

"Again, exactly. They can't claim trial strategy about what they actually *did* together with an adversary, unless they admit they had an agreement for joint presentation. And they can't admit that, because that's exactly what we'll be trying to prove."

* * *

Once again, Jimmy Coleman sat at the desk beside his inlaid Italian chest, looking out at the city, with Jennifer Lowenstein facing him.

"Robert Herrick has called to set up a time for taking my deposition."

"Can he do that?"

"Yes. I'm tempted not to respond so that he has to send a notice and subpoena, but all that would do is delay it."

"You'll just say that there was no agreement."

"Well, yes. I can say that in response to some of the questions. But Herrick knows things. You can see from the Motion for New Trial, where he says that I gave a yellow stickie to Sammy right before jury selection."

"I think I'd tell a little white lie and say that didn't happen."

"Too risky." Jimmy smiled and shook his head. "The bailiff saw us. And also, Herrick has sent Sammy a deposition notice, too. That sorry piece of human wreckage named Sammy Stubarsky, he couldn't stick to a story if his life depended on it."

"Oh. Okay. Well . . . . What do you plan to do?"

"Get stuck in a long trial and have the judge, in that trial, order that I am in attendance at his court and his court only, and I am not to handle any other business."

"Can you do that?"

"I think so. I'll tell the judge in the other trial that Herrick wants to take a long deposition that will require me to take off from that long trial for three days' preparation plus a couple days' worth of deposition, and I'm being harassed by other lawyers who want to set depositions against me too."

"And the judge won't let that happen. He'll issue an injunction against your doing that. Which is exactly what you want."

"Right. And I know exactly which case. That *Continental Motors* case in Austin. The one involving the rollover car accident, where our good client manufactured the car. That's a case I'd like to try, and the judge will give us our injunction."

"We're close to settling that case."

"Not anymore. Jennifer, get us set up to try the *Continental Motors* case. Austin, here we come."

32

What do you mean, he's got strict orders not to give a deposition?" Robert sat under the floor-to-ceiling windows bordering his office. Hearing this strange explanation, he jerked his eyes from the misty gray horizon, from the greensward of Buffalo Bayou, from the crowded freeways outside.

"Mr. Coleman's in trial in the *Continental Motors* case." The voice came from one of Jimmy Coleman's army of associates, who Robert was sure was wearing a black suit.

"Well, he can carve out a half hour for this deposition."

"No, he can't."

"What?" Robert's eyes had narrowed.

"The judge in the *Continental Motors* case doesn't want that trial to be interrupted. And so he's issued an order to all the lawyers telling them they cannot, quote, 'participate in any other proceeding in any manner' during the trial of that case."

"I've never heard of such a thing." Robert sat rigidly in his chair.

"Me neither. But there it is. You can't depose him. Doesn't matter whether you've ever heard of it or not."

"Is it a long trial?"

"It's going to be a very long trial. It's a case about a rollover accident. Nobody knows how long. Maybe six months."

Robert exploded. "Is this something Jimmy Coleman cooked up to avoid testifying?"

"That doesn't sound like Mr. Coleman. He's been a witness before. He's not afraid of it."

But the associate sounded as though avoiding being a witness was exactly what Mr. Coleman had done.

"And so," Robert said slowly, "what you're saying is that Jimmy Coleman won't provide a half hour deposition because he's under orders from another court."

"You got it."

"What do you think the judge in our court, Judge Manny Lopez, is going to think about that?"

"This time, you got me."

"Goodbye," said Robert, as courteously as he could. It wasn't this guy's fault. It was Jimmy Coleman's.

* * *

Sammy Stubarsky wasn't nearly as skillful at avoidance as Jimmy. Two days later, he sat in Robert's office, at the big conference table.

"Now that you've been sworn," Robert said firmly, "you represented two parties in the trial of *Grant v. Blackminster Construction Company*. Isn't that right?"

Sammy smiled. "Yes." He looked like he was hung over. Or maybe drugged. Probably was, Robert thought.

"Did you make any kind of agreement with Mr. Jimmy Coleman during that trial, that involved trial strategy?"

"No." Another smile.

"Did you have what is colloquially known as a wink-and-nod arrangement to coordinate strategy?"

"No." Now, Sammy looked like the cat that ate the canary.

"Did you conform your trial strategy to fit that of Mr. Coleman?"

"That's privileged. You're asking me, now, about my trial strategy, and that's privileged."

"Did you make your trial strategy fit an unspoken understanding that Mr. Coleman would reciprocate by helping your clients?"

"That's privileged. Trial strategy."

Robert threw up his hands. "If I ask you about an agreement, you deny it, I guess because it was silent. If I ask you about an understanding, you claim it's trial strategy."

Sammy just sat there and smiled.

Finally, he said, "That's not a question. Are you through with this deposition?"

"No. Let me ask you this, and it's not about trial strategy, but about what you said and did. Before the jury was selected, did an incident happen with a small piece of paper, which may have been like a yellow stickie?"

"Yes."

"Did this incident occur in the back hallway to the courtroom?"

"I think so."

"What did Mr. Coleman do, and what did you do, during this incident?"

"He did something very unusual. He stuck out his hand, and he was holding a yellow stickie, and he said, 'Sammy, here.' And without even thinking, I took the stickie."

"What was written on the stickie?"

"Three numbers."

"Did you interpret those numbers to be numbers of potential jurors that Mr. Coleman wanted you to strike?"

"Objection. Privileged. Trial Strategy."

"Did those numbers fit some of the potential jurors?"

"Yes."

"Did you, in fact, strike those potential jurors off the jury, whose numbers fit the numbers on the yellow stickie?"

"Yes."

"Looking at these potential jurors objectively, wouldn't you say that these were good jurors for a plaintiff?"

"Objection. Privileged."

"Mr. Stubarsky, that is not a question about your trial strategy. It is an objective question about the potential jurors you struck."

"Okay. The answer is, some aspects of their profiles would favor the plaintiff, and some the defendant, like most jurors."

Sammy smiled. He seemed to be having a good time, and why not? His clients had done well in this case and he'd earned a big fee without doing much.

"You represented two plaintiffs, Mr. Stubarsky. Wouldn't you want to strike the jurors who were worst for the plaintiffs?"

"If you're talking about imagining an average case, I suppose so. But I had my trial strategy."

The deposition went on for two more hours of this kind of sparring.

"So, Mr. Stubarsky. After all of that, after so many instances that helped the defendants rather than the plaintiffs, do you still claim that you had no understanding with Mr. Coleman during this trial?"

"Yes, sir. No agreement."

Sammy smiled.

33

I t is unusual for a hearing on a Motion for New Trial to involve live testimony. Judges usually don't have time for that, and they want to decide these Motions on the basis of documents, including depositions if they're absolutely necessary. But on this occasion, Robert Herrick wanted to present at least two live witnesses.

"Can't it be done without that?" Judge Manny Lopez was almost pleading.

"Your Honor, the testimony will be short. Less than fifteen minutes total, from my side. And I don't think there will be much cross-examination."

The judge's chin was resting on his hand: almost on the bench itself. "Very well."

"The plaintiff first calls the bailiff of this Court."

"The bailiff?"

"Yes, your Honor."

Two minutes later, Judge Lopez saw the relevance of the bailiff's testimony. He intervened to ask questions himself.

"So these two guys, Mr. Coleman and Mr. Stubarsky, passed a note between them with writing on it?"

"Yes, Judge."

"And from what we understand, Sammy Stubarsky got the numbers of jurors to strike from Mr. Coleman, and he struck those jurors?"

"That's my understanding."

"A plaintiff struck jurors that the *defendant* wanted to remove?"

"That's my understanding."

Judge Lopez's head was no longer near the bench. It was shaking vigorously.

"I pass the witness," said Robert Herrick. If the judge is doing my job for me, he thought, I don't want to interrupt.

Sammy Stubarsky passed the witness with no questions. He looked like someone who was trying to find a piece of jungle to hide under.

The black-suited associate who had come to court in place of Jimmy Coleman stuttered a few times, paused, and then passed the witness too.

* * *

When the dust had settled and the bailiff was comfortably off the witness stand, Robert said, "Just a few more minutes of evidence, your Honor."

"You have another witness?" Judge Lopez asked. He almost sounded like someone who wanted to ask, Why do you need another one?

"Yes, your Honor. All of it will be less than fifteen minutes, including the last witness."

"Proceed."

"Plaintiff Grant calls Professor Perry Jones."

Most of the time that the Professor was on the witness stand was consumed by a recitation of his credentials. Longtime law school professor, teaching litigation procedure. Nicknamed the "Father of Tort Reform" in this state. Author of several articles about dealmaking and cooperation among attorneys on opposite sides of lawsuits.

Then: "Professor Jones, what information about this case have you studied?"

"The entire record, from the suit papers through the verdict. Also, the deposition of Mr. Stubarsky. And I've heard the testimony today, too."

"What is your opinion, Professor Jones, about whether Mr. Stubarsky and Mr. Coleman reached a silent agreement about the handling of the trial?"

"The evidence of their having an agreement is overwhelming. They had an agreement. They just kept it silent so that they could deny to the Court that they had an agreement. They had a kind of fig leaf, by doing it without words, so that they could claim that there wasn't an agreement, without thinking they were lying."

"But they had an agreement?"

"No question about it. I call this agreement a 'no-deal-deal,' because the lawyers can claim they didn't have a deal when, actually, they did. Or, they think they can claim that. They think it's not lying."

The trial judge intervened. "Okay, it's less than fifteen minutes, Mr. Herrick. I'll give you that. But let's stop here. I assume Mr. Stubarsky and the Booker and Bayne lawyers don't have any cross examination of this witness either."

It wasn't a question. The opposing lawyers both mumbled, "No, your Honor."

"The Motion for New Trial is granted." Judge Lopez's face was stern. "Mr. Herrick, please prepare me an Order."

"Yes, your Honor."

"Gentlemen, I want this case settled. I'm sending you back before a mediator again. Mr. Herrick, also prepare me an order to send everyone back to mediation."

The judge's voiced, now, sounded like thunder. "And here's an incentive to you to be generous, defendants. The Rules of Evidence allow a party to prove facts about obstruction of justice. Stuff like destruction of evidence, hiding witnesses, stuff like that. And also, fraud upon the court. The person who had those things done to him can show it to the jury, against the party who did it."

The bad news was slowly dawning on the black-suited Booker and Bayne associates. The verdict the defendants had won was erased, now. If they didn't settle the case, there would be a new trial. And also, the new trial would include evidence like the bailiff's testimony about the yellow stickie, the expert opinion of Professor Jones, and the deposition of Sammy Stubarsky. Which was on videotape, and it showed every smirk.

Evidence, in other words, about what the judge called the "fraud on the court" would be admissible at the new trial. The jury would know all about it.

"That's it. Adjourned," said the judge. And everyone stood as he strode down from the bench.

34

Jimmy Coleman's call came through Robert's telephone at eight o'clock the next morning.

"Hello, Robert." The concrete-mixer voice still rasped as usual, but it was less hostile than Robert remembered it.

"Hello, Jimmy."

"I got a report that Judge Lopez ruled in your favor on the Motion for New Trial. Serves me right for not being there, but I'm in trial out of town."

As if your being there, Robert thought, would have made any difference. But he just waited for Jimmy to say something that mattered.

"Next time, Judge Lopez would try this case in a way that wouldn't be kind to me, I guess." Jimmy sounded not just less hostile, but even subdued.

"That's right."

"For now, what we're ordered to do is to mediate the case. Again. But I'd just as soon settle it right now, if we can."

"Sure. Let's settle it. But at a little higher figure."

"Oh, yes. I understand that. But we have a structural problem about that."

"A structural problem?"

"Right. At a certain point, it doesn't make any sense to Blackminster Construction to settle it, because they'd be bankrupt."

Again, Robert waited.

Finally, Jimmy got to the point. "We can offer seven million. That's all the defendants have to spare without massive layoffs. And they don't want to lay their loyal workers off. Besides, if they lay many

175

people off, they don't have their companies. Then, they couldn't do anything."

It's the best defense there is, Robert thought. There are lots of different kinds of defenses, ranging from "I wasn't at fault" to "Your client caused it." And those can be good defenses.

But the best defense of all is, "Even if you win at trial, I can't pay whatever it is that you win." In other words, the best defense of all is, "I'm broke."

"We'll provide you with financial statements." Jimmy was more forceful, now that he had Robert's attention. "And those statements will show you what we have."

"A profit-and-loss statement, as well as a balance sheet?"

"And a cash flow statement, if you want that."

"Audited?"

Jimmy hesitated. "We don't have audited financials, I don't think. Remember, it's not a public company. But here's what we'll do. I'm pretty confident about the financials. We'll include a clause in the settlement papers saying that you've relied on the financials. And it will say that if you discover that they're inaccurate, you can void the settlement."

"Not as good as having a solvent accounting firm pass hands over the balance sheet, Jimmy. Last thing I want is to have to void the settlement and start all over."

"You and me both."

"So . . . ."

"So, we'll do it. We'll get a financial firm to look at the docs and do an audit letter. We don't have time to do a full audit, you know. I mean, we can't get a firm to count every shovel and verify every account receivable."

"I know. Well . . . which firm are you thinking about?"

Jimmy started chuckling to himself. "Maybe Arthur Andersen."

Robert laughed too. "Great idea." They both knew that Arthur Andersen didn't exist anymore, because of its legal troubles.

Even harsh enemies in a knock-down, drag out war can exchange a minute of weak humor when they agree on a peace treaty.

"It's up to my clients," Jimmy went on, "but I'll try to have them get one of the big four accounting firms. If we get anyone else, we'll run it by you beforehand."

"Okay." Robert was satisfied. "Subject to that, and subject to all the other usual clauses in settlement documents, I will recommend the seven million to my client."

Jimmy was in a rare mood, a generous mood. "You did one hell of a good job for you client, Robert."

* * *

"Thank you." William Grant was ecstatic. "Thank you, Robert. Thank you."

"Congratulations to you, Little Willie."

The man in the wheelchair laughed. Robert had avoided using the nickname while the lawsuit was still a bloody battleground. It seemed appropriate now.

"Well, yes," Little Willie said. "Thanks to you, Robert, I can live again."

Once again, for the thousandth time, Robert thought about the emotional toll of litigation. Sometimes, having a lawsuit hanging over your head, even if you're winning, is worse than losing.

* * *

But it was Assistant District Attorney Maria Melendez who had the last word. "Robert, my love, this proves the truth of a lot of sayings."

"How's that?" He had learned to listen to his wife on matters of philosophy, whether deep or shallow. He had a feeling this one was not going to be deep.

"They say that politics is the 'Art of the Possible.' And it's true. But it's even more true of litigation in court."

"Yes. And what we did . . . was . . . , what was possible."

"And they also say, 'Half a Loaf Is Better than None.'"

"Yes. They do say that."

"And in this case, Robert, you got more than half. You got close to three quarters of a loaf. Three quarters is even better than half a loaf. You, big shot, may think you are some kind of a fine trial lawyer. But you'd do better to be humble."

He waited.

"And you ought to go to church and say profuse prayers of thanks," she said, "because you came out better than I ever thought you would."

Postscript

I wanted to write this novel so that the lawyering was real.

In a work of fiction, the story should be more exciting than real life. It's supposed to grab you, the reader, and pull you along. And make you want to turn the pages. But the events in a lawsuit don't always happen in exciting sequences of amazing occurrences. Real lawsuits are real life, which has a lot of boring moments. Still, I wanted this story to be an authentic reflection of the way that a big lawsuit unfolds.

I've used my experience in and out of courtrooms to do this. For example, the kind of agreement that Jimmy Coleman strikes with Sammy Stubarsky actually can happen in a lawsuit. More on that later. The suit papers, the depositions, the jury selection, the evidence, the jury arguments, and the court's instructions and questions to the jury are all realistic.

But I've included this Postscript because the demands of fiction always pressure the writer. They make a writer simplify things beyond most reality, and they make for what sometimes is called "dramatic compression." A role that in life would be played by multiple people is shoehorned into one character. A sequence of events that in life is tedious, long, and boring, but that must be treated meticulously, gets shortened.

This Postscript will help you to separate what is real from what is fictitious.

* * *

The seven million dollars for which Robert and Jimmy ultimately settle is a pretty high figure. But it's at least possible, in a situation like this one, where a high earner loses the ability to work, his life is no longer normal, and he will have very high medical expenses. Usually, a plaintiff settles at a discount from the ideal verdict, because the case doesn't need to be tried to obtain a judgment. A trial is always chancy, and the discount reflects that. A jury isn't exactly as random as a roulette wheel, but it's more like that than most people would like to think. For the same reason, the defendant pays a higher number of dollars than the defendant would think is ideal.

The frequency of trials today is lower than ever. Ridiculously low, one might say. The last figures I saw showed that civil jury trials in federal court were about one and a half percent of the cases. Trials are rare. Furthermore, they usually come about because one side or the other has misjudged the case. One side has made a mistake about how good the chances are. As a result, there usually are a clear winner and a clear loser in a trial.

And that may be one reason why there are so few trials. Lawyers become expert at guessing how well they will do in a trial. But there are other reasons. Trials today are longer, more complicated, and more expensive than ever. The rules of the game are unpredictable sometimes, and they create traps, and no lawyer who is a professional wants to gamble with a severely injured plaintiff or, on the other side, a low probability bet-the-company defense. There's no case that can't be lost. There are very few slam dunks. And there's another reason why there are so few trials. Since trials have been dwindling, there are fewer lawyers than ever who know how to try a case!

I recently talked to a big-firm lawyer from New York, where trials are notoriously few and huge, well-paid firms do very little in the way of trial work. I asked, "So, what do you do when your firm faces the fact that it's going to have to try a case?" He said, "We hire a stand-up trial lawyer." I hope there are enough of those to go around.

I tell my law students that even if trials are fewer than ever, you need to study how trials work. There are three reasons. First, you don't know how to evaluate a case for settlement if you don't understand how it will be tried. Second, if you have no idea how the case is going to be tried, your opponent will know about your ignorance, and you won't get fair settlement value. Third, there will come a day, even if the number of trials is in the one percent range, when one of your cases will go to trial. You are better off if you can try it, or, if you must get a "stand-up trial lawyer" late in the game, you can prepare it so that it can be successfully tried.

A lot of people bemoan the infrequency of jury trials. It feels as though something is wrong, if we never, or almost never, try cases. Trials drive settlements; it is the ability to predict what might happen at trial that enables the lawyers to settle their cases. And that is as it should be. But if there are so few trials, how do we know?

But I expect there to be ever fewer trials. The way we would increase their number would be to simplify our procedures, shorten the time of trial, and reduce the cost. There are lots of suggestions about that, but very little action. And there is an army of law professors out there who write articles that almost inevitably involve more complexity. Many of them have never tried a case.

* * *

In this novel, the case itself and the source of the injuries to the plaintiffs are realistic. I can't swear to all of the medical analysis, in spite of my research, because I'm not a gastroenterologist, and I can't guarantee everything about the handling of the construction details for the same reason, but I can say that the injuries would present in this manner and be treated in the litigation system this way. I actually had a case in which the plaintiff was severely injured by a construction crane that split his gut, just like the injuries to William Grant.

We settled it.

* * *

There are several technical elements that are required in suit papers in my state, but that are not included in the suit papers that Tom Kennedy prepared. For example, the first paragraph would include a statement that would restrict or expand the scope of discovery—how many depositions there would be, for example. The statement would say something like this: "Plaintiff alleges that this case belongs at discovery level 3." That simple sentence would designate the case as a large and complex one, and it would have various consequences during the litigation. At first, I put that statement in the document, but later I decided I shouldn't include technical items like that.

The plaintiff's lawsuit document is called a "petition" in my state, as it is in some other states, so that's what Tom files. More commonly, in other places, it's called a "complaint." Every state has different rules about it. The statement that the suit involved more than $1 million is also there for technical reasons. It's needed, in my state. And there would be a sentence that shows the jurisdiction of the court, in a form that complies with the rules, but I didn't include it.

Another item that I put in, and later took out, was a reference to a rule that lawyers know as *res ipsa loquitur*. The sentence read this way before I removed it:

"Plaintiffs invoke the doctrine of 'the event speaks for itself,' or, in Latin, *res ipsa loquitur*, because the crane was in the defendant's exclusive control, and the occurrence was of the type that does not normally occur without negligence."

This rule makes it a little easier for the plaintiff to prove the case, especially when no one knows exactly how the accident happened. A competent plaintiff's lawyer would include this rule in a petition or complaint in a case like this one.

The idea behind the rule is exactly what it says. In Latin, the rule is called *res ipsa loquitur*, or translated, "the event speaks for itself." In other words, the evidence lets us infer that this accident must have been caused by negligence, even if we don't know precisely what the act of negligence was. It requires proof that there was a mechanism or process under the control of someone, and it caused injuries that normally wouldn't occur without negligence. There would have been some controversy over whether it fit this case, because there are two defendants who had a part in the crane. But the controversy probably would be up to the jury to resolve. I included this rule in the suit papers at first, but then I removed it, again because it was a little too technical.

* * *

Incidentally, this involvement of two defendants would have created a conflict of interest, and they should have had two separate lawyers. Blackminster's best defense might have been to blame Janowitz, and vice versa. But maybe both of them wanted Jimmy Coleman, and he got them to waive the conflict. And I needed dramatic compression: fewer characters.

On the subject of Jimmy Coleman, he might be thought of as a caricature. One of my reviewers, a lawyer with a wonderful reputation, said, "I have never met a Jimmy Coleman." Well, I haven't met lawyers exactly like Jimmy, but he combines characteristics that some lawyers do exhibit. The insults, the dirty tricks, and the intimidation are part of the game to some lawyers, unfortunately.

One part of my story that I actually disagree with is the depiction of the big law firm as more prone to cheat than the smaller one. Big law firms are not sleazier than little ones, at least in my experience. Maybe the fact of being a part of a large organization makes the lawyers meet at least a basic standard of integrity. But people seem to like a story where a little guy fights a big organization, and the public seems to think that big firms are worse. I guess in this story I've fostered that idea, which I consider wrong, except for my having included this paragraph.

* * *

Speaking of two defendants, you may have noticed that there were two plaintiffs in the suit papers that Tom prepared. There was William Grant, of course, and there was also Delores Grant, his wife. If a husband is injured by someone else's negligence, his wife is injured too; and it works in reverse if a wife is injured, because her husband is, too. Delores Grant's injuries would have been intangible: loss of companionship and the like.

But the law allows the plaintiff to recover for those intangibles. In damages, or in other words, in dollars and cents. So Tom included her in the petition. But I didn't develop the proof and evidence that would go into her case very much. Dramatic compression, again.

* * *

My story ends in a way that is unfamiliar in courtroom dramas. The case settles.

Perry Mason always tries every case. It's not very realistic, even back in the day when we tried a few more cases. A real Perry Mason would settle most of his cases. Since he handles criminal cases, he would plea-bargain most of them.

"Plea bargaining" has a distinctly negative sound to it. But it's just a synonym for settling. In criminal courts, district attorneys screen the cases, and they should aim for a guilty-verdict percentage of 85 to 90 percent. A lesser guilty-not guilty percentage means that the district attorney's office is wasting resources—scarce and precious resources, because a jury trial is a precious resource—and harassing possibly innocent people. A higher percentage means that the prosecutors are not trying difficult cases. They are avoiding hazardous duty, such as the trial of the one-witness rape or robbery case.

Perry Mason never loses, either. He never has to collect fees from his clients. He has an in-house investigator. And he manages, in most cases, to get the real killer to confess on the witness stand. (I've never seen that happen.)

Because this novel doesn't involve collecting a fee, and Robert Herrick presumably would have, let me remedy that oversight. Robert would have had a written fee agreement with his client. It might have provided that any recovery without trial would entitle his firm to a fee of 33 percent; any recovery involving any trial or partial trial, 40 percent; and a recovery after an appeal, 45 or 50 percent. And the expenses (such as expert witnesses) come from the plaintiff's share. If there's no recovery, there's no fee.

Why is it so expensive? Because we Americans have built the most expensive system of justice in the world. Less than half of the dollars spent on personal injury lawsuits go to injured people. The costs of handling the litigation are more than half.

* * *

At the beginning of the lawsuit, Robert Herrick wonders whether it can be filed locally. Or whether it has to be filed in Alaska. This question depends on decisions by the United States Supreme Court. The decisions are not very clear. In fact, they're badly written, and they're below any standard we should expect in our Supreme Court.

In one of its recent cases, the Court had to decide about a lawsuit filed in a state other than the one where the accident or dispute happened. This was the issue Robert faced: an accident that actually occurred in Alaska, but a lawsuit that he wanted to file in his home state.

The issue can be important. Sometimes it becomes the most important battle that the parties fight. The state where the suit is filed may have been chosen because it's the one where the plaintiff thinks the population will give the most damages, when they serve on a jury. Sometimes it's a question of avoiding big-time inconvenience, such as a suit in Alaska conducted by lawyers from the lower forty-eight.

The Supreme Court's opinion that gives the answer isn't very good, as I've said. In fact, it's terrible. The Court said that, if an incident happened in one state, and you want to file suit in another state, you can do it only if the defendant is "essentially at home" in the state where you file suit. That's what our exalted Supreme Court wrote. So, if you sue a company, you have to figure out where that company is "essentially at home," even if it's a far-flung corporation that has its "home" everywhere.

What the heck does that mean? Exxon Corporation would seem to be "essentially at home" in all fifty states, because it has major decisionmakers everywhere, and besides, it's bigger everywhere than most one-state businesses anywhere. But maybe the Supreme Court's opinion means you can sue Exxon only where Exxon has its headquarters, over an event that happened elsewhere. (And of course you can usually file suit in the state where it happened, but in many situations, like the suit in this story, it would be silly for you to do that.)

In Robert's situation, with the case for William Grant, the question had a relatively clear answer. All of the defendants resided or were headquartered in the state of suit. So he had to consider the question, but it was easy to resolve.

Meanwhile, there are many cases in which the answer isn't clear at all. Parties to lawsuits waste huge sums of money fighting over what the Supreme Court meant, while knowing that in the end, they may have a judgment that is worthless. But being a Supreme Court Justice means never having to say you're sorry.

* * *

There's another aspect of this story that has produced a lot of questions.

Do plaintiffs and defendants actually make agreements like this "Judas-lawyer agreement," or do they cooperate, so that they can pin the blame on other plaintiffs or defendants?

The answer is yes, at least in some states. I have a friend who believes that, in a personal injury case like the one in this story, it is malpractice not to attempt to make a deal of that kind.

The kinds of agreements vary tremendously. One type is the "*Mary Carter Agreement*," named after a long-ago case in which the Mary Carter Paint Company was a party. The plaintiff sues multiple defendants. Then, the plaintiff settles with one defendant, but keeps that defendant in the case. Assuming that the plaintiff gets a favorable verdict, the settling defendant gets part of its money back.

The incentive of the settling defendant, of course, is to become an advocate for the plaintiff. The courts tried to level the playing field by disclosing Mary Carter Agreements to their juries. But the settling defendant and plaintiff made that solution less workable by writing an agreement that contained all sorts of gruesome details of the plaintiff's injuries and heaped blame on the target defendant.

Today, Mary Carter Agreements are illegal in my state (and every other state that I know of).

The agreement in the lawsuit brought by William Grant, and formed by Jimmy Coleman and Sammy Stubarsky, is not a Mary Carter Agreement. There is no agreement to reimburse any defendant. That means it's not a Mary Carter type, and it's not outlawed.

But the parties to the agreement are required to disclose it. When the court inquires, or a party inquires before the court, it is illegal, not to mention foolish, to deny an agreement if one exists. Jimmy and Sammy took the position that "We don't have an agreement," because they had exchanged no explicit terms of agreement. Their position was that each lawyer pursued his own trial strategy, and the fact that it happened to be parallel did not make it an agreement.

I call this variation a "No-Deal Deal." To me, it's obvious that there is, indeed, an agreement, but it's hard to prove.

* * *

Do lawyers really maneuver their cases as vigorously as Jimmy did, to try to get a favorable judge?

Yes, although usually not in the way Jimmy did it. I've illustrated this possibility on occasion by picturing a case in which the plaintiff's attorney has the option of filing suit in either a state court or a federal court, and the attorney can also structure the suit so that the defendant can't change the choice. Imagine that the plaintiff's attorney helped the federal judge to get his appointment, so that the federal judge is presumably favorably inclined toward him. The plaintiff's lawyer, then, structures the suit so that the federal court has jurisdiction. Or, imagine that the lawyer gave a big campaign contribution to the state judge in the last election. Now, the plaintiff's attorney shapes the suit so that the case is filed in the state court and the defendant cannot change it.

All perfectly legal.

In most cases I think judges try hard not to give in to the favoritism that these attorneys want. But even so, many judges have reputations for favoring either plaintiffs or defendants. And attorneys act accordingly in trying to get their cases in front of favorable judges.

The method that Jimmy Coleman used in this story is illegal, of course. It isn't proper for a lawyer to trade with a cohort in the clerk's office to defeat a random case assignment system. I doubt it can be done in precisely the way I've written it here. I wouldn't want to give anybody any ideas. But not too long ago, the Supreme Court in my state disciplined a group of lawyers who found a way to rig a random assignment system (a different way).

* * *

You shouldn't get the impression from this story that a Motion for New Trial is often granted. It's actually pretty rare. The reason is as is stated in an earlier paragraph of this Postscript: a jury trial is a precious resource. We can't try a high percentage of cases. If we wanted to, we'd have to have multiples of the number of judges that we have today.

And there is a kind of ethic among trial judges, to defer to juries. I've tried cases to judges without juries and heard the judges occasionally think out loud about what a jury would do in a similar case, as a kind of guide to their own decisions. A few years ago I read a story in a lawyer newspaper about a retiring judge who proudly said that in twenty-plus years he had never granted a new trial.

A new trial is probably more likely in a case in which the judge believes that there has been a "fraud on the court," as Judge Lopez thought in this case. But I think judges actually try hard not to be influenced by lesser kinds of misbehavior, or at least not to overreact to it. Sorting out misbehavior raises side issues that distract from the main case and sometimes are hard to get clear evidence about. Most judges would like to think that they could continue presiding over a jury trial impartially. But there are types of dirty tricks that are more serious, like the defendants' behavior in my story.

* * *

The depositions that I've described are realistic, and so are the tactics that they feature. The method of jury selection is what you would see in a real case. The evidence is realistic, and so is the questioning at trial.

All of that is shorter than it would be in real life, of course. I've presented excerpts from those procedures. Dramatic compression.

One of the evidence issues that has prompted people to ask questions is the judge's announcement that the facts about the "fraud on the court" will be admissible in the retrial that will result from the Motion for New Trial. I don't know how any particular case would come out if it involved this question, but the principle is accurately stated. Since time immemorial, the rules of evidence have allowed proof of your opponents' attempts to defeat justice illegally. So, destroying evidence, hiding witnesses, or untrue answers in discovery, can usually be shown to the jury.

A judge might extend this idea to evidence of an illegal agreement that requires a new trial. I hesitate to pronounce this as a certain or likely outcome, but it fits. My hesitation comes from several sources.

First, the judge might or might not find that an agreement existed. The judge might be persuaded by Jimmy and Sammy's reasoning.

Second, the evidence of impropriety in this case would be complicated—more complicated than proof of, say, destruction of evidence. The proof could easily become a trial within the trial, lengthening the whole process and distracting from the ultimate issues. The sideshow might take over the circus, so to speak. Judges have discretion to exclude evidence that causes this problem.

* * *

There's a question that arises in all of my stories, and it's about the emotional response of Robert Herrick to the prospect of a trial. He's nervous. Not just nervous, but scared. Readers have puzzled over this, because they think that since he's a professional, he would approach a trial with a calm mind.

Not necessarily. Some of the best trial lawyers have to resist the urge to go to the bathroom and lose their lunch on the morning of a trial. It's a very personal battle. One person is going to lose (unless both lawyers lose, which can happen). And that's a personal defeat. You've misspent years of preparation, and the jurors didn't like the way you handled it in front of them—or, maybe, didn't like you. You'd have to put any caring about the consequences out of your mind to be cold-blooded. You'd have to avoid worrying about your client who's in a wheelchair and depending on your performance in combat, to have a calm mind.

There are trial lawyers who are fearless. They are sometimes the same people who, if they didn't get stress from trials, would get it somewhere else. They would go gaming in Las Vegas at the high roller tables or drop thousands of feet before opening their parachutes. I don't know how I got into it, or how I stayed with it, because I am decidedly not that type.

Instead, I was the type who was scared before trying a case but went ahead and did it. Like many others who do that kind of work. Just ask a trial lawyer!

— David Crump
2016

Also by David Crump, in the *Robert Herrick Series*

Sudden Death Overtime

The Target Defendant

Murder in Sugar Land

The Holding Company

Conflict of Interest

Introducing David Crump's
The Target Defendant

1
THE MOTION TO DISMISS

Judge Marvin Raines frowned. "So, Mr. Herrick ... why shouldn't this court dismiss your lawsuit? I mean, throw it out?"

Judge Raines glared at the plaintiff's lawyer, adding, "The Bank is your target defendant. The Velnikov Bank. But your claim against the Velnikov Bank doesn't involve any of the actual killers, and the Bank just did what banks always do. It took in deposits, and it lent money. . . .

"So, why shouldn't I grant the Bank's Motion to Dismiss?"

Robert Herrick's shirt was soaked with sweat. He visualized that gory building that the press had come to call "The Death House." He imagined the dead children, and he could see the blood on the walls.

The Velnikov Bank was responsible. The bank managers' stamp was on this crime just as much as the hired killers'. And the judge was about to throw out his clients' only chance for justice.

The Bank was going to get away with it.

He kept his voice even. "Judge, the Velnikov Bank took in money from depositors who actually had nothing. And then parceled it out to layers of fake borrowers that were controlled from inside Mexico. The Bank laundered money for the Balamarcas Drug Cartel."

Robert stretched his six-foot-two height upward to face the judge. Women jurors always found themselves attracted to Robert when he denounced a negligent company, with his striking blue eyes and with the shock of dark hair over his forehead. The men were impressed with his ability to speak without notes at the end of a long case and to admit the weakness in his evidence, without showing weakness.

His pinstriped suit was charcoal gray: the lawyer's uniform. His dotted tie was of the quality that symbolized success, worn by a man rich beyond imagination. But none of this mattered, because the bloody scene from six months ago flooded his mind.

"Judge, what this Bank did was essential to the operations of the Balamarcas Drug Cartel."

"But did the Bank know that? How could the Bank have known?" The judge's head was bald and shiny, and his eyes were deep brown, almost black. Above the black knot of the tie that tucked into his black robe, his mouth was set. Judge Raines was tough on lawyers, and right now, he looked downright scary.

Jimmy Coleman was Robert's arch rival. He stood up on the opposite side of the courtroom, representing the Bank. "That's right, Judge. Nothing's unusual about a bank having depositors that it also lends to! That's the normal banking relationship."

Jimmy slapped his hand on the table. "Judge, this is the most deserving Motion to Dismiss that you're ever going to see!"

Jimmy Coleman was the head of the trial section at the mega-firm of Booker and Bayne, where an army of associates cranked out briefs to justify every harassing tactic he thought of. Normally, a dismissal was a long shot, but this Motion was supported by a dozen complicated arguments, conjured up by Jimmy's legions. Now, Jimmy's dirty grin was a mocking insult.

"Judge Raines, what this Bank did is not the normal banking relationship." Robert made himself speak confidently. "The Bank received millions of dollars from fake depositors who had no net worth, no personal fortunes. And they shifted the money through layers and layers of shadowy, empty-shell businesses. And these were the same fake businesses that helped the Cartel—the Balamarcas Cartel—get its drug money back to Mexico. The Velnikov Bank laundered money for drug dealers."

"It *laundered money?*" The judge looked at Robert with a mixture of curiosity and rejection. "But the Bank's not responsible if its people didn't know! Again, how can you say that the Bank knew?"

Robert struggled to get his point across. "The Bank immediately turned around and lent the money to another group of people and businesses, and federal regulations forced it to collect their financial statements." He pointed at the Bank's officers. "These managers knew they were lending to fake borrowers, just like the fake depositors, and they used layer upon layer of empty-shell businesses to funnel the money to the Balamarcas Cartel. It's money laundering."

"Now that ... that's just Mr. Herrick's speculation!" Jimmy sounded like sandpaper on concrete.

"Right away, the money made its way back to the Balamarcas drug lords."

"Without any action by this Bank!"

Robert shook his head. "Judge, we—the plaintiffs—have an accountant who will testify. And he will trace the money trail. It could not have happened by accident. Our accountant will show how the Bank worked together with the Balamarcas Cartel."

"An accountant can't salvage this lawsuit!" Jimmy's voice grated like hailstones in a canebrake. "This is the kind of speculation that the Motion to Dismiss was designed for."

Four other lawyers from Booker and Bayne sat behind Jimmy, each billing hundreds of dollars per hour. These black suits were overkill, because Jimmy was the only one who spoke. But the Booker and Bayne associates all smiled and nodded, now, to let everyone know how silly Robert's lawsuit was.

"Well, I understand your arguments." Judge Raines touched his laptop, and the ceiling lights reflected from his mirror-like scalp. "I'll let you know my ruling soon."

He hesitated. "But I can see that I'm in for a hindsighter in the court of appeals no matter what I decide." The judge let a tight smile show. "Oh, well. Those appellate judges can overturn my decision, but they can't make me read their order."

The lawyers both laughed politely at the judge's witticism, and they sat down.

* * *

After the judge left the bench, there were rustling sounds, as lawyers stuffed too-thick documents into too-small satchels and scrambled toward the door.

The Bank President stood up along with Jimmy Coleman. His name was Chola Velnikov: the Founder of the Velnikov Bank. He wore a purple suit with pinstripes, a purple shirt, and a purple tie—together with orange shoes. Purple and orange were his trademark. His white hair was cropped in a kind of burr cut, and his eyebrows grew together.

The purple-suited man had beamed like a lighthouse upon hearing the judge criticize the plaintiffs' case. He was still smiling.

Robert looked at his partner Tom Kennedy, the lawyer he worked with most often. Tom's voice was reassuring. "I have a good feeling. The judge can't grant the Motion to Dismiss if he follows the law, and Judge Raines is smart enough to know it."

Jimmy Coleman waddled by them. He carried a map of his life on his face, punctured by eyes so pale and dead that witnesses turned away when he cross-examined them. "Herrick, I almost hope the judge lets this piece-of-shit case of yours go ahead, because I'd like to try it in front of a jury. They'll dump you right out onto the street."

The black suits all giggled, and one of them said, "But the judge is going to be merciful and dismiss this worthless suit."

Booker and Bayne had offices in Washington, New York, London, Frankfurt, Moscow, and Tokyo, as well as Houston, and the associates were famous for heaping scorn on their opponents. Especially opponents who had sensitivities, like buttons that could be pushed.

Robert waited while the black suits passed by. Then: "Tom, I hope you're right about having a good feeling. Because I don't feel good at all."

And both of them thought back to the day when this lawsuit had begun, six months earlier. They thought about the bloody house, the death house, and the mayor's press conference. And they both thought, "How could this have happened?"

It was Tom Kennedy who finally broke the silence. "How could these murders have been committed in a civilized country? How could something happen, like what happened six months ago?"

2

SIX MONTHS EARLIER

The mayor trudged down three steps toward eager members of the press. The circle of microphones looked like the claws of predators in the blinding sunlight of August. Everywhere, cameras clicked. The building that the press had already begun to label "The Death House" was a black hulk behind the mayor.

Robert Herrick followed quietly. His face was pale and tight.

Dozens of shouted questions rang out, all at the same time. "How many bodies, Mr. Mayor?" . . . "Who did this?". . . "Is it one family or more?"

Feedback sang in one of the microphones, and then it was quiet, and the mayor spoke. "I'll make a short statement, and I'll take a few questions. There's a lot we don't know yet. This is going to be a long investigation. I know you understand: we just do not want to speculate at this early time."

There was a murmur from the circle of reporters. It told the mayor that on the contrary, the press wanted to hear some speculation.

"First, let me say that our hearts go out to the families of these unfortunate people who were taken from us. One of them, as you know, was a distinguished journalist, and we are all grateful for his excellent work. That's Rafael Castillo, the newspaper reporter. Our thoughts and prayers are with him and his family. We will not rest until this horrendous crime is solved."

The mayor raised his voice. "There are eight deceased persons inside this house. They include two children whose ages we do not know, but one is a toddler. There are three men and three women. Frankly, this is the ugliest crime scene I've ever seen. . . .

"The homicide division is inside now, investigating. Their work will include everything from photographs and videos to collecting blood and vacuuming for hairs and fibers. They will leave no stone unturned. And you can be sure of this: we will find the person or persons who did this and bring them to justice."

The mayor looked up at the sky and paused.

"At this time, our fine police department is keeping an open mind about this event. Every potential scenario is on the table, even the possibility of a murder-suicide situation. We do not know whether it is a crime committed by many individuals, or just one. We do not know whether it is a revenge killing, or carried out for some other criminal purpose. We do not know yet what weapon was used, or whether there were multiple kinds of weapons.

"And that is as much as I can tell you, now. We don't want to speculate, and I can take your questions, but I have to warn you: I probably won't be able to answer some of them."

The mayor was sweating more than the weather should have required. His eyes were wet. Even the reporters, who were not accustomed to feeling sympathy for politicians, could understand his stress.

The first question came from Channel 2. "Mr. Mayor, from what you're saying, it sounds drug-related. Is that one of the possibilities that the Police Department is considering? That this is a drug crime?"

"I can't confirm that. The investigation will go where it goes, and there are many possibilities." But the mayor's contorted face told the assembled reporters that the answer was . . . Yes, the mayor did think that this was a drug crime.

Channel 13 spoke next. "Do you have an explanation, then, that seems like the most likely motive for this event, yourself?"

"Well, I suppose I have theories within my own mind, yes, just as anyone would have."

There was a pause. The press waited, expecting the mayor to tell the world what his "theories" might be.

"But I cannot tell you anything about any theories!" The mayor's voice carried a hint of exasperation. "Remember, we aren't going to speculate at the earliest stage of this critical investigation. We aren't going to speculate."

Again, there was a pause. The reporters seemed to hope that the mayor would slip, somehow, and say something speculative, in spite of his determination.

And they hoped it would be quotable.

Finally the Chronicle broke the silence. "Mr. Mayor, can you tell us what this crime scene is like? I mean, you said it was the most brutal you've ever seen. Can you describe it and tell us why you'd say that?"

The mayor looked up, and the lines in his face grew deeper. He was a skillful politician, but he floundered, unable to describe this sight. The silence lasted, and then, there were murmurs from the crowd of journalists.

Robert Herrick whispered an answer. "There is blood. And more blood. There is blood on the walls and even on the ceiling." He was trying to help the mayor verbalize it.

The mayor reflected for a moment before deciding that he could say this. And that it would not be unwise to say it.

"There is blood. A lot of blood. There is blood on the walls and even on the ceiling."

The mayor's face tightened again. "The individuals standing behind me, ladies and gentlemen, are of course our excellent police chief and also Mr. Robert Herrick. Some of you may know Mr. Herrick as the well-known Lawyer for the Little Guy, and he has also been one of my trusted outside advisers. I am grateful to Robert Herrick for answering the call and consulting with me about this horrific crime."

Under the circumstances, Robert was surprised about being mentioned, particularly as a "trusted adviser." He mouthed the words, "I'll always be here, Mr. Mayor," and he added, ". . . whenever you call."

Meanwhile, it seemed that the detail about the blood on the ceiling had done the trick. It was the kind of lip-smacking shocker that the press wanted.

"I will leave it to the police chief to give you further information." The mayor turned and walked, at least figuratively, "offstage," and the reporters turned their attention to the police chief. Robert Herrick silently followed the mayor's lead. The mayor flopped onto the back seat of his long black car, and Robert joined him.

It was nine o'clock in the morning, and already it seemed like a long day.

* * *

Later that same day, Robert sat motionless in his office, with an unseeing stare.

Tom Kennedy, Robert's most trusted partner, was having trouble getting the boss's attention. "Robert, you need to work on your argument against this Request for Summary Judgment in the *Molinari* case. It's set for tomorrow. You know, the Summary Judgment the defendants want the judge to grant against us, in our lawsuit about that truck accident. The *Molinari* case."

He waited. Then: "Robert, I know you were called by the mayor this morning, and you walked with him through that crime scene. But this *Molinari* case is a completely different thing, and it's important too. It's set for tomorrow."

Robert Herrick's office was at the top of the Chase Tower. The tallest building in town. The floor-to-ceiling windows were built in a greenhouse style, and today was a beautiful sunny day. To the south, the downtown buildings rose up in spires of brown, gray, and white. To the west, Memorial Drive wound busily alongside the bayou. Its greensward pointed toward Memorial Park and then disappeared into the haze of the horizon.

"You need to work on your argument in that truck accident case," Tom repeated. "The *Molinari* case. To keep our lawsuit alive." He sat in front of Robert's big mahogany desk, in one of the three desk chairs.

The office was spacious. The furniture was spare but elegant. The dark parquet floor was covered by the most beautiful oriental carpet Kennedy had ever seen, with squares, crescents, circles, and diamonds in every color. Below the windows, a hundred geraniums bloomed in shades of red, pink, and white. But neither Robert nor Tom saw any of it right now.

"I'm . . . just not up to working on another case, after what I saw this morning." Robert's anguish was as though he had known all of the victims personally. "Eight innocent people, once living, . . . now dead. I realize, sometimes I identify with the people too much. But when it comes to thinking about a completely different case, even one that's set for tomorrow . . . I'm not up to it."

"I know you're not up to it. And I understand why. But our clients in the *Molinari* case are counting on you."

"I know. . . . Hey, Tom, how about this? Do you think you could argue this *Molinari* case tomorrow? . . . Instead of me?"

Tom had to crane his neck around a two-foot-high stack of accordion files on Robert's desk. Suddenly, he realized that all of this paper was from one single case: a pro bono suit for a small corporation that had been left bankrupt after a much bigger corporation had breached its contract. The whole office had spent hundreds of hours on this case, even though it was a likely loser, because Robert thought the client was right.

"Me, argue the *Molinari* case?" Tom's voice signaled his incredulity. "Normally, yes, but in this case, no. And you know why. It involves all kinds of engineering details about the truck, and I don't know anything about it. I'm just your coach."

"I know." Robert gazed idly toward the wall, where paintings by Mondrian, Picasso, and Wyeth hung in a row. The success of the law firm of Robert Herrick and Associates had been phenomenal. Once a one-lawyer operation, it had more than twenty attorneys now, all working for injured plaintiffs and small businesses.

There was a pause. Kennedy started to say something urgent about the clients in the *Molinari* case but thought better of it. "I realize that the death house scene this morning is affecting you, Robert. The mayor is lucky to have an outside advisor like you. An advisor who gives him straight advice."

"Tom . . . do you think . . . we could do something about the murders I saw this morning? To help that Castillo family's relatives, and to stop this kind of killing from happening?"

Kennedy sat bolt upright. "Robert! Come down to earth. We're civil lawyers. We can't do anything, not in a million years. The murderers may never get caught, and if they do get caught, they won't have any money to pay a judgment with, even if we sue the pants off of them."

"Well, that's right. I was just thinking. . . . And . . . Well, you're right. I need to focus."

Robert's weakness, Tom Kennedy always said, was thinking too much about what might be ideal. Thinking too much about right and wrong, unconnected from practicalities—and not thinking enough about finances. Still, he had to admit that the growth of Robert's practice had been amazing. Robert Herrick and Associates had more than a hundred employees, including an audio-visual studio that made exhibits and videos for use in court. And all of it had been built by Robert himself, after he had graduated from law school with nothing but debts. He had refused the big salaries offered by every big firm in town, because he'd wanted to go it alone.

Now, his firm handled large and small commercial cases along with large and small personal injury cases, almost always on the sides of individuals or mom-and-pop companies. The big-firm lawyers treated him with respect, especially when they agreed to settlements in the millions of dollars. His clients loved him, because he felt about their injuries the way they felt. He never left it to the bloodless pages of the law books.

"You're . . . right, Tom. Let's get to work on that *Molinari* case."

Several hours later, with plenty of commands from Tom to stay on the subject, Robert Herrick finally pronounced himself ready to defend against the Summary Judgment tomorrow. He poured two fingers of very good scotch from the bar in the corner of his office. And drank it too quickly. Then:

"I realize it doesn't have anything to do with the *Molinari* case, but Tom . . . do you think . . . there is any prospect that we could do anything about this massacre at the Castillo home? And about stopping all the drug murders that will probably come in the future?"

Tom shook his head. He always wanted the firm to represent more banks and insurance companies, the kind of clients who could pay the bills, but he never succeeded in persuading his senior partner.

"We can't do anything about the crime scene you saw this morning, Robert. Not in a million years."

3
EL JEFE

E l Jefe, the Boss, looked out over the Sierra Madre Mountains and felt a warm, flowing spread of contentment.

There were three parts of his job that were tricky. But this event in Houston, these eight killings, helped move two of them past a cloudy uncertainty. It was nice to have Rafael Castillo dead, and all of his family.

El Jefe's "job" was to be the invisible hand behind a huge drug empire, the Balamarcas Cartel. One of the difficulties he faced, of course, was getting his sales inventory into the United States—his cocaine and heroin. But that was only his most obvious problem. The second issue, over and over again, was getting his money back from the United States. It had to be laundered first and consolidated into new cash, and then it usually had to be driven by trucks into Mexico in large bills, hidden in shipments of machines and computers. Electronic transfers were too likely to get intercepted by the DEA—the Drug Enforcement Agency. Old-fashioned vehicles were slower, but safer.

The other tricky part of his business was getting some kinds of murders done. Murders were an important part of the business. And the hardest ones to manage were the killings that were a long way away, especially in the United States, with hit men he didn't know. It wasn't that El Jefe felt anything about the people he ordered killed. It was a matter of getting it done right, with pride. El Jefe knew that when it came to his management of people, his image was as important as his business ability or his innovations in cruelty.

"*Bueno*," said El Jefe to his First Lieutenant, a man named José Luis Leyva. "Good. We've got those *gusanos*, those maggots, finally dead. Those *gusanos* from the newspaper."

"The *gusanos* in North America?" Sometimes it wasn't easy for José Luis to keep up with all of the groups that were candidates for execution.

"The *gusanos* that were in the way, yes. Disrupting our operation. Cutting into our money."

El Jefe was a man of cultured tastes, and he knew how to live well. This palace, balanced on a leveled space at the top of Colina del Pescador, his hill, let him see for a hundred miles. He lived in a ten-thousand-square foot space that had an indoor pool, an indoor shooting range, and a multi-million-dollar view. This was one of El Jefe's five houses, which were spread across Mexico, Costa Rica, and Argentina.

"Don't ever forget, José Luis, that people who spread lies about us are bigger enemies than the other Cartels, even the Marietas Cartel or the Escondidas Cartel. Journalists like Rafael Castillo are more dangerous than our competition. He was one of those news hacks who call us names and try to get the army on our backs. Rafael Castillo wrote a lot of ugly stories about the Balamarcas Cartel, and these killings were all about that. We've finally shut him down."

"Well, *Jefe,* the publicity you have put out across Mexico about the charitable operations of our Balamarcas group, our band of soldiers in this state, has been a gift from God. That's one reason our governor, our friend, visits us here at Colina del Pescador, your home."

"That, and the money, and the women. The governor likes it all." El Jefe smiled with his teeth, and he laughed.

El Jefe's black hair was slicked straight back on both sides of his broad flat face. He favored military fatigues, but they were always elegantly tailored and crisply starched. Here in his own drawing room, he wore a dress shirt with small brown camouflage spots and a green camouflage jacket with bigger spots. His trousers, sharply creased, matched the jacket. His feet were adorned with elegant brown loafers with unusual shapes, because they were made by Gucci and sold for hundreds of dollars.

El Jefe was what everyone called him in public, but his given name was Alejandro Carlos Gonzales-Huerta. Some people used his nickname: *El Más Loco,* or "The Craziest One," but rarely to his face. On the wall behind him, as he sat looking through the enormous plate glass windows in his drawing room, he kept his display pistols: relics and historical weapons. Even a gun formerly owned by Emiliano Zapata. There were two pistols that were gold-plated, and assorted other rarities. Each one rested on an elaborate individual shelf so that El Jefe could take it down, hold it, and feel it.

He favored classical music, and right now the smooth strings of Beethoven's Sixth Symphony began to weave their magic. El Jefe, or *El Más Loco*, threw his head back and enjoyed it. Maybe he was The Craziest One, but he knew music.

"The greatest composition ever written for an orchestra!" Alejandro-The-Craziest-One told José Luis. "I'm sure you know, José Luis, that this Beethoven symphony is the one they call *The Pastorale*, with bass lines that are supposed to sound at first like sun on the meadow. And then, they blend into musical thunderstorms."

"Of course." José Luis did not know, or care, about this masterpiece, but he knew enough to go along with *El Más Loco.*

El-Jefe-The-Craziest-One listened, just listened, to the symphony for a full minute before he moved. Then, he stood up and stretched his legs. For the thousandth time, he spotted the famous words that were painted in big letters over the door to this luxurious room. He read them aloud, in the original Latin:

"ODERINT UT METUANT."

And with that, for want of a wider audience, El Jefe turned to his lieutenant so that he could show off his knowledge of history, language, and culture. "José Luis, it is said that this was the motto of the Roman emperor Caligula. *'Oderint ut Metuant.'* And it means: *'Let everyone hate me, so long as they fear me.'* That's the translation."

El Jefe stretched his arms, now. "Today, they describe Caligula as the most brutal Roman who ever lived. Here's an example. Emperor Caligula once ordered his soldiers to push a whole section of spectators sitting in the Roman Colosseum onto the performance floor to be torn apart by lions, because there were no prisoners available for the purpose."

José Luis had heard it before, but he wisely pretended to be interested.

"Actually," El Jefe went on, "Caligula was a most capable manager. He knew how to lead people, and they did what he wanted. And do you know what, José Luis? His motto fits us, too. So I say it, right along with Caligula: *Let everyone hate me, so long as they fear me.*"

El-Jefe-The-Craziest-One smiled with satisfaction. He listened in silence to Beethoven before he spoke again. About business.

"José Luis, be sure that our partners who killed Rafael Castillo and his family are compensated beyond whatever the contract is. They have served our Balamarcas Group well, by getting rid of these *cucarachas.*"

El Más Loco was nothing if not generous.

* * *

"I've never seen anything like those murders in that house." Robert Herrick sat with his wife in his living room, where the sunlight filtered through plantation shutters. "Not even in Viet Nam."

"It sounds unbelievable," agreed Maria Melendes, who was an assistant district attorney. "I've seen murder cases, but this sounds like one that tops them."

"The worst to see was the baby. Probably two years old." Robert looked toward Maria. For the thousandth time, he thought about how beautiful she was, with her huge almond eyes below her ringlets of red Hispanic hair. And with the pale, almost translucent skin, that showed her Cuban heritage.

Maria closed her eyes. "It had to be a drug deal gone bad. They're the only ones who do this kind of thing. I mean, killing everybody in the place, whoever happens to be there, at random, including babies who can't talk. It's a way of making their point by killing everyone."

"It had to be several people who did it, all organized, because the folks who lived there were armed. They were heavily armed. And the killers must have used guns to subdue all of them. But the murders— they were done with cutting instruments. Maybe a machete. That's what it looked like."

"Look there." Suddenly, she pointed at the television.

The screen had filled with pictures of the local news anchors, plus the weatherman and sportscaster, all wearing toothy smiles. Quickly, the camera focused on the man in the center. "Good evening, friends! I'm John Moreno, and This . . . Is . . . Action News!"

The anchor dropped his smile. Obviously there was unpleasant news to come. "The city's police force is investigating a multiple homicide on the southwest side."

Maria sat up. "Robert, this is about what we were . . . just discussing. The horrifying scene that you and the mayor saw."

John Moreno's voice rose. "For the first time, we are learning about the victims. One of them was Rafael Castillo. He was a twenty-year news reporter who did major service to this region. He broke the city hall scandal of two years ago, and he uncovered corruption in Enron Corporation before that. His most recent work was a series of articles on drug gangs from Mexico, such as the Balamarcas Cartel. About how they operate north of the border. He showed us all that the drug lords have their fingers here, in our city, much more than most people think."

The pictures shifted slightly as John Moreno smoothly turned to another camera. "This city is a major drug transshipment point, kind of a drug-gang clearinghouse for the entire country."

"So . . . the reason this entire family was killed was drugs? To shut a news reporter up?" Maria said it firmly.

"Wait. We don't know for sure, yet."

"I know." She was shaking her head in disgust.

The news anchor continued his explanation. "But Rafael Castillo was not the only victim. The dead include his wife and his children. And there were also his parents. The father and mother of Rafael Castillo. Neighbors say the parents did not live there. They just visited often."

"Yes, and they were in the wrong place at the wrong time," Maria whispered.

This was going to be one of the longer television news stories. A so-called "two-minute epic." Two minutes sounds like a short time, but it becomes a long time on the screen. Veteran newspeople will tell you that it takes a number of scene changes—actual footage of an event, or interviews, or the like—to keep viewers watching for two minutes without pushing the button on the remote.

"The Police Department has provided video of the scene at the death house," John Moreno announced breathlessly. "We warn you that these are graphic images, not suitable for all of our viewers."

The scene shifted to a hallway leading into the home. The camera panned downward from the top of a two-story entrance. Then it turned left, to show the body of a man. Part of the image had been blocked. Even with John Moreno's warning, and even with its taste for guts and gore, the television station had qualms about showing this footage. The path of the camera continued, and then it centered on the body of a woman, also edited.

"Rafael Castillo and his family." John Moreno's voice was somber. He kept up a running narrative during the rest of the camera's trip through the house, but at times he just let the video speak for itself. He was silent, for example, when the camera briefly showed the body of the murdered toddler.

"It's sensational, but I'm actually glad they're doing this," Maria said. "I see this kind of thing at the DA's office. Only a few jurors ever see it. But the entire public ought to witness how ugly murders are, without the editing, so that in this fine democracy, they can vote intelligently. Such as voting for more people who are concerned about crime."

Robert nodded. "A lot of people think of murder as a clean thing, like what Agatha Christie writes about."

"That's right. They do. But instead, it's dirty."

Maria Melendes knew what she was talking about. She lived it on a daily basis. She was an assistant district attorney, and she had an unusual job. When a convict received a death sentence, it was her responsibility to follow up. The death sentence meant nothing by itself; it always would be followed by a long chain of appeals and petitions for habeas corpus. In fact, there would be multiple loops through the habeas process. Maria's gut-wrenching task was to represent the state in pursuing the execution of the death sentence, often through more than a decade, and sometimes more than two decades, of hearings, briefs, motions, arguments, and rehearings, until the end.

Sometimes, there would be eleventh-hour claims of innocence—or of recently developed mental retardation, because the Supreme Court has told us that it is unconstitutional to execute the mentally retarded. Then, it was Maria's responsibility to evaluate these claims quickly, and sometimes, to agree with them. Or to oppose them, vigorously, as incorrect. It was a job that required more judgment than was ever comfortable.

Her responsibilities earned Maria an informal title. Everyone called her "The DA's Official Killer." She carried a Prada purse; she loved stuffed animals; and she traveled back and forth to the Walls Unit of the Texas Prison system, to see that executions were carried out.

Now, on television, John Moreno was ready to wrap up the Death House story. "Funeral arrangements will be made on the coming Monday for Rafael Castillo and his wife." And there was a sterner part of his finish. "One angle that the investigators are pursuing, we're told, is the possibility that this set of killings was an effort to silence Rafael Castillo." The anchor's voice was angry, now. "This has mobilized the police force, because it is a short distance from murders that silence the truth to the breakdown of democracy."

It was an unaccustomed lapse of editorial comment during a hard news broadcast, but perhaps forgivable.

4
THE CLIENTS

As soon as Robert Herrick stepped into the foyer of his law firm, the associates wanted to know the result of the hearing he'd just finished.

"Boss, how did the *Molinari* case go? That case about the truck collision?"

"Robert, did it come out right?"

His answer to each one was the same. "The judge didn't decide. He'll let us know soon. I can't see how he can throw out our case, but I can't make predictions."

Eventually, he made it back to his corner office. Donna DeCarlo stopped him.

"Robert, you have clients. The mayor sent them."

"What?" And then he realized. These probably were the clients he had wished for when he had talked to Tom Kennedy. Probably, they were relatives of the murdered journalist, Rafael Castillo. But at the same time, he dreaded meeting them, because he knew he couldn't help them.

He opened the door. A man and a woman, both elegantly dressed, were standing there. "Hi. I'm Robert Herrick."

"Mr. Herrick, I'm Patrick Castillo. I'm Rafael Castillo's brother."

"And I'm Anna Castillo Carter. Rafael's sister. Mr. Herrick, you were with the mayor when you went . . . to my brother's home." She hesitated. "We appreciate your . . . visit to . . . the place where he died."

"I'm so sorry for your loss. More so than anyone can imagine."

Patrick Castillo was fumbling for words. "I, I appreciate your visit too, Mr. Herrick."

"How can I help you folks? What can I do?"

Patrick shook his head. "We're not exactly sure. But we don't want to sit on our hands. We'd like to . . . do something. Something that the law will let us do."

Robert was sympathetic, but he had to tell them. "Well . . . we're all civil lawyers here. We don't know how to get someone arrested or prosecuted. The police department is pulling out all the stops to solve this case. To catch whoever did it. And I'm sure the DA's office will have the same attitude when the perpetrators get caught."

"We know about that, yes. We're here because we want to use the civil law. We'd like to sue the people behind it. The drug lords . . . who hired the killers."

"Come, sit down, please." But the reason Robert said it was that he needed to sit down himself.

"Suing a drug lord who's probably in another country? And connecting him to the murders? That's . . . beyond anything I know how to do. Even assuming you could persuade a court in this country to exercise jurisdiction over a drug lord who's in a foreign country."

Robert thought for a minute. "Let me ask you. Is there a security company that patrols that area? We could look into whether there was a lapse in the security. And possibly sue the security provider. But I doubt it would be a good lawsuit, and this firm does not file lawsuits that don't have evidence behind them."

"We know your reputation." Patrick Castillo's voice was quiet. It was also full of pain. "But we know there must have been people or companies here in the United States that helped the drug dealers. And we'd like to do something about that."

"People or companies . . . Like . . . Who?"

"We . . . don't know yet. We hoped that you . . . you could find out."

Robert knew the answer to that. A lawyer can try, and he can hope, but trying to find a shadow defendant to sue is not what a lawyer is good at.

"Well, maybe we can . . . put an investigator on it." Robert knew he sounded doubtful.

I ought to just say no, he told himself. It would mean less heart-break in the end, for both the lawyer and the clients.

"We . . . would appreciate that." Anna Castillo Carter was the one who said it. "Thank you. Thank you."

She sounded as though she thought that this nice lawyer, Robert Herrick, was going to hurry to file a lawsuit that would stop drug violence for all time. At that, Robert felt an even heavier dread.

* * *

At the top of his mountain, Colina del Pescador, El Jefe spoke with a restrained kind of anger. "The governor called me. The *Federales* came to pay him a visit. You and I can do fine, if we have to deal with *Los Federales*. But the governor can't."

"Yes, that's a problem for the governor," José Luis answered softly.

El Jefe wore his usual uniform: a starched camouflage shirt under a green camouflage suit, with shiny Gucci shoes. He looked like a guerilla ready to conduct jungle warfare, except that it was all perfectly pressed.

"The governor depends on the Federal Government in Mexico City. If it were us, if we were having to deal with the *Federales*, we would give them what we call *la mordida*: a little morsel of a bribe. And the *Federales* would go away. But it's harder for the governor."

"What seems to be the reason for the *Federales*' visit, *Jefe?*"

"A bunch of unimportant people got killed in a bar near *la playa,* the beach." El Jefe frowned. "These dead people were nobody. Nothing."

Since the victims were unimportant, it annoyed El Jefe to have to think about this incident. Or to have the *Federales* nosing around. Why would they do that? For dead people who weren't important?

José Luis turned a strange color. He flinched. El Jefe noticed, and José Luis saw that he noticed.

El Jefe's voice changed. "One of the people who got killed was a young woman from Durango. The daughter of someone, I don't know who yet, in that Cartel. Our enemies, or at least our competitors, that particular Cartel. It amounts to a big pile of nada, a bunch of nothing, as far as I'm concerned, but the *drogistas* in that part of Durango are mad at us about it. They're really angry."

"And so . . . ."

"And so, the *Federales* want to try to convince the Durangans that it wasn't us who killed those people. Now, I know how these things are, when you're celebrating. It's hard to celebrate without killing a few people, especially women."

"That's right, and a few days ago . . . it was Fifteenth of Septiembre." José Luis brightened. El Jefe would understand, even if he was also known as *El Más Loco*.

September 15 is the night before Independence Day in Mexico. The celebration starts then. It begins with *El Grito*, or The Outcry, by the President of Mexico, who rings a bell and breaks out with a loud yell. The assembled multitude erupts with praise for heroes—*Viva Zapata! . . . Viva La Virgine de Guadalupe!*—and also, the people shout their condemnation of the bad guys, especially Spaniards, of course, because the Spanish were the villains from whom independence was won. The official Day of Independence is September 16, but for the most determined revelers, the night before is the proper time for drunkenness and violence.

El Jefe smiled. "Well, okay . . . so everyone was out celebrating Independence Day. Not just our people, but the whole city. Anybody could have killed those people in Hemosillo. I guess that's what you're trying to tell me, José Luis?"

"*Exactamente*. It . . . it wasn't us." José Luis's voice wavered, ever so slightly. "We didn't do it."

"This isn't a time to lie to me." El Jefe turned away, toward his red and black billiard table, with its marble-and-gold billiard balls.

The subject was closed. José Luis knew it. Uncomfortably, he backed out of the room. . . .

The Target Defendant, available in paperback and eBooks at leading booksellers and online sites.

Visit us at *www.qpbooks.com.*